On What We Owe to Each

On What We Owe to Each Other

Edited by
Philip Stratton-Lake

Blackwell
Publishing

© 2004 by Blackwell Publishing Ltd

First published as Volume 16, number 4 of *Ratio*

BLACKWELL PUBLISHING
350 Main Street, Malden, MA 02148-5020, USA
108 Cowley Road, Oxford OX4 1JF, UK
550 Swanston Street, Carlton, Victoria 3053, Australia

First published 2004 by Blackwell Publishing Ltd

Library of Congress Cataloging-in-Publication Data has been applied for

ISBN 1-4051-1921-7

A catalogue record for this title is available from the British Library.

Set by SNP Best-set Typesetter Ltd, Hong Kong
Printed and bound in the United Kingdom
by MPG Books Ltd, Bodmin, Cornwall

The publisher's policy is to use permanent paper from mills that operate a sustainable
forestry policy, and which has been manufactured from pulp processed using
acid-free and elementary chlorine-free practices. Furthermore, the publisher ensures
that the text paper and cover board used have met acceptable environmental
accreditation standards.

For further information on
Blackwell Publishing, visit our website:
http://www.blackwellpublishing.com

CONTENTS

INTRODUCTION*

In this volume various eminent moral philosophers assess aspects of T. M. Scanlon's seminal work *What We Owe to Each Other*[1] (*WWO*), and Scanlon responds to the issues they raise in Chapter 7. In this introductory chapter I shall outline the main lines of Scanlon's account of what we owe to each other, and indicate the ways in which he has modified his view since the publication of *WWO*. This will hopefully provide a useful point of departure for the critical essays in this volume, and Scanlon's response to them.

At the heart of *WWO* is Scanlon's contractualist account of a central aspect of the morality of right and wrong. But since this account builds on his view about the nature of practical reasons, it is useful to start with the first three chapters of *WWO*, where Scanlon lays out his account of practical reasons and their relation to value and well-being. In chapter one he argues that practical reasoning is best understood in terms of reasons rather than desire. In chapter two he rejects a teleological conception and defends a buck-passing account of value. And in chapter three he argues that there is no non-moral notion of well-being that enables it to function as a master value.

Consequentialism is never far from view in Scanlon's discussion of these topics, and the positions he rejects in the first three chapters have implications for consequentialism.[2] If the desire-fulfilment theory of practical reasoning is correct then deliberation will focus on what is instrumental to bringing about the state of affairs the agent most desires. Deliberation will, therefore, focus on ways to bring about certain (desired) outcomes. If the teleological account of value is true, then the only appropriate response to the good will be to produce as much of it as possible.[3] And since one's overall well-being is a state that is to be

---

* I am indebted to Rahul Kumar, Michael Ridge, and T. M. Scanlon for extremely helpful comments on an earlier draft of this Introduction.

[1] All unattributed references are to this work.

[2] This aspect of his view should not, however, be exaggerated. See his Chapter 7, 127.

[3] Scanlon points out the converse implication, namely that 'if rightness is a matter of promoting the good, then the good must be the kind of thing that is "to be promoted"' (81). He also goes on to point out that the appeal of the teleological account of value is not limited to consequentialists.

brought about, focusing on well-being will lead us to understand all values in terms of reasons to bring about certain results (133). Consequentialism may survive if these views about reasoning, value and well-being turn out to be false, but it will be deprived of an important source of nourishment.

Reasons

Scanlon distinguishes a reason in the basic normative sense, from an agent's operative reason (19). An operative reason is what an agent regards as a (normative) reason, and a normative reason is a consideration that counts in favour of some 'judgement sensitive attitude'.[4] Judgement sensitive attitude's are complex dispositions to think and react in specific ways (21), dispositions which aim to track the relevant normative beliefs. The relevant normative beliefs are beliefs about reasons to adopt some attitude. Judgement-sensitive attitudes are thus attitudes an 'ideally rational person would come to have whenever that person judged there to be sufficient reason for them and that would, in an ideally rational person, "extinguish" when that person judged them not to be supported by reasons of the appropriate kind' (20).

If we focus on operative reasons, it may seem as though reasons are psychological states, such as beliefs or desires. But in the standard normative case, reasons are typically not psychological states, but facts or propositions. My reason for not buying the shirt is not my *belief* that it is day-glow pink, but that it is day-glow pink (although this consideration would not motivate me unless it figured as the content of one of my beliefs) (56).

Many philosophers believe that desires have an important motivational and normative role. Scanlon rejects this view. Normally, a person's judgment that she has sufficient reason to do A is an adequate explanation of her forming the intention to do A. There is no need to invoke any source of motivation apart from this

---

[4] We seem to have reasons to act, and actions are not attitudes. Scanlon tries to accommodate reasons to act by claiming that:

> Actions are the kind of things for which normative reasons can be given only in so far as they are intentional, that is, are the expression of judgement-sensitive attitudes (21).

Scanlon seems here to be saying that there *are* reasons for actions as well as for attitudes, but that there are reasons for action only *because* actions express attitudes. This seems to go against his general thesis that reasons only ever favour attitudes.

judgement (34). We can be motivated to different degrees depending on how forcefully we are made to appreciate the reason-giving force of some consideration, but getting us to appreciate this is not conjuring up an independent desire (34–5).

Scanlon also rejects the view that desires have a fundamental normative role. Many of the reasons we have depend upon what we desire, but the fact that we desire something is almost never a reason to pursue it. Our reasons are provided by the features of things that make them good. These good-making features may simply be future pleasure, or they may involve some prudential or moral consideration (42ff). But because of his buck-passing account of value, Scanlon would deny that the fact that something is good provides a reason in addition to the features of that thing that make it good. (I outline Scanlon's buck-passing view below.)

Furthermore, desire-based theories cannot account for a common and important structural feature of deliberation. Deliberation is not merely weighing up the strengths of conflicting desires. I may judge one consideration (C) to be a reason for taking another consideration (D) not to be relevant to my decision whether or not to pursue a certain line of action (51).[5] This process is not deciding between the strength of competing desires, but is a decision about whether some consideration is to have any weight at all, eg, whether the fact that a certain shot will win me the game in tennis will be a reason to go for it. I may decide that this fact is not a reason, as I'm trying to build up the confidence of the person I'm playing. Similarly, in an interview situation in which my friend is an applicant I might decide that the fact that he is my friend will not count as a reason to appoint him. The reason provided by our friendship is not merely outweighed in this situation, but is *excluded* from consideration.

The reasons we have are not to be explained with reference to desire. On the contrary, desires are to be understood with reference to (what we take to be) a reason. In *WWO* Scanlon argues that to desire X is to regard some feature of X as a reason. Since the publication of *WWO*, however, Scanlon has weakened this claim. He now thinks that the account of desire in *WWO* was overstated, and tended to over intellectualise desire.

---

[5] See also J. Raz, (1999, ch.1).

> In habitual action, for example, we carry out what are some-
> times quite complicated sequences of actions while hardly
> being aware that we are doing so. Given this lack of attention,
> it is rather implausible to say that in carrying out these actions
> we are aware of various considerations as reasons (2002a, 340)

The notion of the reasonable plays a central role in Scanlon's contractualist account of the morality of right and wrong. He defines the reasonable with reference to his account of reasons. The reasonable is, he maintains, what we have reason to do or think 'relative to a specified body of information and a specified range of reasons, both of which may be less than complete' (32). I may be unreasonable by ignoring something relevant that I know, or by ignoring relevant information of which I am igno-rant, but that is nonetheless available to me. Alternatively, the reasons relevant to reasonableness may be relative to certain aims, e.g. a concern for others, or for scientific progress (33). As we will see below, the reasons relevant to the morality of what we owe to each other are those that are relative to the aim of mutual recognition.

Value

We have seen that, for Scanlon, there is a very close connection between reasons we have to desire, admire, pursue, or in general, to care, about certain things and the value of those things. How, then, is value to be conceived? In chapter two Scanlon rejects one dominant conception – the teleological account of value.

According to the teleological account of value, the primary bearers of value are states of affairs, and for a state of affairs to be (intrinsically) valuable is for it to be 'to be promoted' (79–80). On this view, then, good things are states in which certain things exist, and the only appropriate response to the good is to bring as many of these things into existence as possible.

Scanlon argues that the teleological account distorts the way in which we understand value. The primary bearers of value are not states of affairs in which, say, friends and scientific knowledge exist, but rather friendship and scientific knowledge themselves, and the response of promotion is seldom the appropriate response to these goods. To think of friendship as valuable is not to think of it as something that is to be promoted. We would not, *ceteris paribus*, think it appropriate to the value of friendship to betray one friend in order to acquire two others, either for ourselves or for others (89). Rather, to think that friendship is valuable is to regard reasons of friendship (reasons of loyalty, concern for our friend's interests, keeping in contact, spending time together, etc) as good ones (90).

The same is true of the example of science and scientific knowledge. To think that such knowledge is intrinsically good is to think that people who have the relevant ability have reason to take up scientific enquiry as a career, that those who do have reason to be good scientists, to work hard, to choose significant lines of enquiry, to report the results accurately and treat the results of others fairly, etc. It is also for others to support their work, and for us to think that we have reason to try to understand science and to admire its achievements and those who make them (90–1).

Scanlon proposes a buck-passing account of value.[6] According to the buck-passing account of value, the fact that something is good is not itself a reason to care about it. Rather, the fact that it is good is the fact that some other fact gives us reason to care about it. On this view, then, the only reasons we have to care about the good are the features that *make* it good.

The buck-passing account of value does not imply that if A is better than B, we have reason to respond to A with a stronger pro-attitude than we respond to B. One might think that human beings are more valuable than other animals in virtue of their ability to make rational decisions. Scanlon's view is that this difference gives us reason to respond to human beings in a different way, rather than in the same way but more intensely (2002a, 352).

In *WWO* the reasons Scanlon focuses on are natural properties, such as the property of being pleasant, or of casting light on the cause of cancer (97). But his buck-passing account of value does not commit him to the view that natural properties are the only good-making (reason-giving) properties. 'More specific evaluative properties often play this role' (2002b, 513)[7].

---

[6] The buck-passing view is not to be contrasted with the teleological view. One could be a teleological buck-passer. One would then claim that the good is to be promoted, but deny that the fact that something is good is a reason to promote it.

[7] See also Wallace (2002, 447).

Well-being

In Chapter 3 of *WWO* Scanlon turns his attention to the notion of well-being, and Jonathan Wolff assesses his views on this topic in Chapter 3 of this volume.

One type of reason that is important for Scanlon's contractualist account of morality is reasons relating to individuals' well-being. That compliance with a certain principle will make someone's life go worse is an important ground for that person to object to that principle. Scanlon denies, however, that well-being functions as a 'master-value', that is, that morality can be grounded in a non-moral conception of well-being. On the contrary, well-being is a value that presupposes other values that are independent of it. Many of the things that contribute to well-being (e.g., family and friends, or success in one's rational aims) are valued primarily for reasons other than the benefits they bring to the agent – and some of these reasons may be moral (129). Well-being cannot, therefore, act as a master-value – that is, as a distinct realm of value that can ground all other values. Certain things are not valuable because they contribute to our well-being. Rather, they can contribute to our well-being only because they have value.

What makes someone's life go better? Scanlon rejects the experiential quality and desire-fulfilment theory, and argues for a substantive good theory of well-being. According to this view, there are three things that make our lives go better. The first, and most important, is success in our rational aims. The second is forms of desirable consciousness, whether or not one has aimed at them. *Ceteris paribus* one life is better than another if it is more pleasant. Finally, certain objective goods can make one's life go better.

> "Many goods that contribute to a person's well-being depend on the person's aims but go beyond the good of success in achieving those aims. These include such things as friendship, other valuable personal relations, and the achievement of various forms of excellence, such as in art or science" (125).

A misanthrope who cares nothing for friends could still get some of the instrumental benefits of friendship, but could not get other benefits "that involve standing in a certain special relation to others, since he does not stand in that relation to anyone" (123).

I have described this as a substantive good *theory* of well-being, but Scanlon denies that his view amounts to a theory. A theory would do more than list what things make a life go well. It would provide a more unified account of what well-being is, give an account of the boundaries of the concept, and provide a standard for making more exact comparisons of well-being. Scanlon is sceptical that a theory, so understood, can be provided.

Scanlon's contractualism

Scanlon aims to understand a limited, but central, aspect of the morality of right and wrong in contractualist terms. The sense in which his view is contractualist is not obvious, as the notion of agreement (actual or hypothetical) plays no significant role. Indeed, in her contribution to this volume Onora O'Neill argues that Scanlon's view may be better understood as constructivist rather than as contractualist.[8]

If actual or hypothetical agreement plays no fundamental role in his theory, why does Scanlon describe his view as contractualist? Scanlon calls his account contractualist because of the emphasis it places on what principles others have reason to accept, or reject, and on our reasons for caring about this (Chapter 7, 125).

> The idea of a shared willingness to modify our private demands in order to find a basis of justification that others also have reason to accept is a central element in the social contract tradition going back to Rousseau. One of the main reasons for calling my view "contractualist" is to emphasize its connection with this tradition. (5)

What is fundamental to Scanlon's view, however, is not the non-normative issue of whether others do, or would, agree on certain principles, but the normative issue of whether acceptance or rejection of these principles would be reasonable.

The term 'morality' is commonly understood to refer to a diverse set of values with distinct normative bases. Scanlon's contractualist theory is not intended to cover the whole of morality understood in this broad way. It is intended to cover a central

---

[8] For Scanlon's response to this suggestion see his Chapter 7, 123–125.

aspect of morality that concerns interpersonal relations – that is, the morality of what we owe to each other. His account does not, therefore, relate directly to impersonal values, such as the intrinsic value of preserving the Grand Canyon. Such values only relate to the morality of what we owe to each other in so far as they relate to the experience and activities of rational agents. A principle of environmental indifference would only be wrong in the contractualist sense in so far as it interfered with some worthwhile activity of rational agents, and thus gave those agents a reasonable ground to object to that principle.

Duties to the self are also external to the realm of morality with which Scanlon is concerned (172, 174)[9]. It may be wrong in a more general, non-contractualist, sense to let my talents go to waste, but it is not wrong in the sense that Scanlon aims to describe. A principle that interfered with my ability to develop my talents may be wrong in the relevant, contractualist sense. But this would be because this intrapersonal value would have been brought into the realm of interpersonal value.

Not all interpersonal values are directly relevant to the morality of what we owe to each other. Certain interpersonal values, such as friendship and parenthood, are external to this part of morality.

'Being a good parent, or a good friend, involves seeing the interests of one's child, or one's friend, as constituting reasons for action. These reasons are not plausibly explained by appeal to what would be required by principles that it would not be reasonable to reject (2002a, 349)[10]

Scanlon characterises his contractualist principle of wrongness in various subtly different ways. These different formulations take either a 'permission' or a 'prohibition' version of the principle, though I do not think that either version is supposed to have priority.

According to the 'permitted-by-rejectable-principles' formulation Scanlon maintains:

' . . . in order to decide whether it would be wrong to do X in circumstances C, we should consider possible principles governing how one may act in such situations, and ask whether any

[9]   See also, Scanlon (2002a, 350).
[10]   See also 172ff.

principle that permitted one to do X in those circumstances could, for that reason, reasonably be rejected.' (195)

What does it mean for a principle to *permit* an action? The notion of a permitted act is standardly understood simply as an act that is not forbidden, but a principle does not permit an action by not forbidding it. If it did, then a principle banning gratuitous torture would permit murder for hire, and this is certainly not Scanlon's view.[11] His view seems to be that a principle permits an act if it licences, or authorizes it.[12] So understood, a principle banning gratuitous torture would no more permit murder for hire than my forbidding strangers from walking on my lawn authorizes them to vandalise my car.

According to the 'forbidden-by-unrejectable-principles' formulation deciding whether doing X in C is wrong is deciding whether doing X in C is forbidden by principles that no one could reasonably reject (153).[13]

Some formulations of Scanlon's principle make reference to shared aims or motivations. For example, he writes that his view 'holds that thinking about right and wrong is, at the most basic level, thinking about what could be justified to others on grounds they, if appropriately motivated, could not reasonably reject' (5)[14], and elsewhere he states that, according to contractualism, 'when we address our minds to a question of right and wrong, what we are trying to decide is, first and foremost, whether certain principles are ones that no one, if suitably motivated, could reasonably reject' (189). These references to motivation may make it seem that Scanlon thinks that the moral reasons he is concerned with apply only to those who already care about justifying themselves to others. This is not, however, his view.

Scanlon's view is that moral reasons do not depend upon a contingent desire, but are valid universally (73, 367). But his contractualist principle defines wrongness in terms of what it is

---

[11] See Stratton-Lake (2003b).

[12] See, for example, Scanlon (1998, 203).

[13] Scanlon seems to think that if an act is wrong according to the prohibition version then it will be wrong according to the permissions version of the principle. He writes:

If it would be reasonable to reject any principle that permitted one to do X in circumstances C, then it would seem that there must be some principle that it would not be reasonable to reject that would disallow doing X in these circumstances. (195)

[14] See also 154.

reasonable to reject, and the reasonable relates to a specified realm of reasons. As we saw earlier, what it is reasonable to reject is determined by a range of reasons that are relative to a specified body of information and a specified range of reasons (33). Certain aims and concerns are mentioned in Scanlon's principle as a way of specifying the range of reasons that are relevant to the morality of what we owe to each other. But agents have these reasons irrespective of whether they care about justifying themselves to others.[15]

Scanlon is a pluralist about the grounds of reasonable rejection. I might reject a principle because it licenses actions that put a great burden on me, or because of the effect on my well-being. But the grounds of rejection are not limited to considerations of well-being. I might reasonably reject a principle on the ground that it licences actions that are unfair or arbitrary. These grounds for rejection are not supposed to be exhaustive, but there are certain restrictions on which considerations can count as grounds of rejection.

First, the grounds of rejection must be *personal* reasons.[16] Scanlon's contractualism offers a theory of the part of morality concerned with what we owe to each other. So reasons for rejecting a principle

> 'correspond to particular forms of concern that we owe to other individuals. By definition, impersonal reasons do not represent forms of such concern. They flow from the value of those objects themselves, not (at least in the first instance) from anything having to do with my relation to other people (219–220).

Second, the grounds for rejecting a principle must be what Scanlon calls 'generic reasons' (204). Generic reasons are ones that anyone would have in the relevant circumstances. This rules out considerations based on particular aims, preferences, or other characteristics of specific individuals.

Third, I could not reasonably object to a principle on the ground that it permits actions that I believe are *wrong*, or on the

---

[15]   192. See also Scanlon (2002b, 519).
[16]   Michael Ridge argues that this condition provides the basis of a response to the charge that Scanlon's contractualist framework is redundant (2001). For an alternative response to the redundancy objection, see Stratton-Lake (2003a).

ground that I think the principle is *mistaken*. This would make Scanlon's contractualist principle empty (216). He does not, however, rule out all moral beliefs. As we noted earlier, he allows that more specific moral considerations, such as unfairness, or arbitrariness, can act as grounds of rejection.

A fourth constraint is the individualist restriction. According to the individualist restriction, individuals can only object to a principle on their own behalf (229). These objections cannot be aggregated so that the sum of a small benefit to a sufficiently large number of individuals can outweigh a very great benefit to one person. The sum of the smaller benefits is given no weight in Scanlon's contractualism because 'there is no individual who enjoys these benefits' (230). The individualist restriction allows Scanlon's contractualism to offer a clear alternative to conse-quentialism and avoids the sort of counter-intuitive consequences that follow if aggregation is allowed.

One such consequence is illustrated by Scanlon's transmitter room example (235). Jones's arm is trapped by a piece of electrical equipment, and he is receiving extremely painful electrical shocks. The only way to free him is by turning off the transmitter for fifteen minutes. But this would interrupt a world cup match watched by millions of people, a match that will not be finished for another hour. So if Jones is rescued many people will be deprived of the pleasure of watching the match. If their individual benefits were aggregated then they may outweigh the great benefit to Jones of being spared an hour of intense pain.

It seems, however, that we should not wait to free Jones, no matter how many viewers would benefit by seeing all of the match (235). The individualist restriction supports this intuition, for on this view numbers do not matter. It makes no difference in the transmitter case whether there is one viewer or a hundred million viewers. Since there is no one who would enjoy the aggre-gated benefit, no one could reasonably reject a principle that dis-allowed it.

But if numbers do not matter, then it would seem that they will not matter in cases where the benefits to individuals are the same, and this seems wrong. In a situation in which I have to choose between saving one person (A) or two others (B and C), there would be no reason to save B and C in preference to A. Since the individual benefit to B and C of being saved would be the same as the benefit to A, and we cannot sum the benefits to B and C, it looks as though the individualist restriction implies that I ought either to save A or B and C, but I have no reason to save B and C rather than A.

Scanlon denies that his view commits him to this implausible implication. He maintains that in such a case it would be wrong to flip a coin to decide what to do. If I did this, C could reasonably object that I was not taking his plight into account. For the presence of C would make no difference to what I should do. If I had to choose between saving either A or B, then perhaps I should flip a coin to decide whom to save. If I reach the same conclusion when C is also present, then C could reasonably object that the cost to him of not being saved was not being taken into account. The fact that one of the two could object in this way 'breaks the tie' (232).

Scanlon's way of dealing with the aggregation problem has been subject to a great deal of criticism,[17] and Joseph Raz and Derek Parfit add to these criticisms in their contributions to this volume.[18] Scanlon has recently admitted that his treatment of this issue was the part of the book with which he was least satisfied (2002a, 354). Could he abandon the individualist restriction yet retain a distinctively contractualist theory? Scanlon maintains that he could on the condition (a) that the elements of the revised view 'restrict aggregative arguments, thus avoiding implausible results in cases such as that of Jones and the transmitter', and (b) that 'these elements have a clear contractualist rationale' (Chapter 7, 131).

Scanlon thinks that the alternative that Parfit suggests, or a view very close to it involving aggregation restricted by certain distributive principles (Parfit's Priority View and a qualified form of his Triviality Principle) meets these conditions (Chapter 7, 131–3). If he is right, then the individualist restriction is not as central to contractualism as many philosophers think.

Reasonable rejectability and wrongness

It is natural to regard Scanlon's contractualist principle as providing the most general characterisation of what *makes* certain actions morally wrong. So understood the fact that an action is

---

[17] For criticisms of this view see Kamm, (2000, 348) Otsuka (2000), and Norcross (2002).
[18] Chapters 4 and 5.

disallowed by a principle that no one could reasonably reject would explain, or at least play an important role in explaining, why that action is wrong. Understood in this way, contractualism could agree with opposing theories about what wrongness is, and disagree only about what gives acts this property (10).

Scanlon rejects this understanding of his contractualism. Although he aims to provide a general criterion of wrongness, this is not his chief aim. He also wants to 'characterize wrongness in a way that makes clear what reasons wrongness provides, and this aim goes beyond saying "what makes acts wrong,"' (11).

Furthermore, if his contractualism were understood solely as an account of what makes acts wrong, then wrongness itself would be either an unanalysable, reason-giving property, or a higher-order property 'of violating (some or other) important standards of conduct and therefore being open to (some or other) serious objection' (11). Scanlon maintains that both of these views are unacceptable.

If the former view were correct, then the reason that wrongness provides would be unexplained. If, however, the latter, buck-passing view were correct, then wrongness would not be a reason-giving property at all, and that is, Scanlon believes, implausible. Although Scanlon thinks that goodness can be understood in buck-passing terms, he maintains that wrongness is different.

'In at least a wide range of cases, the fact that an act is wrong seems itself to provide us with a reason not to do it, rather than merely indicating the presence of other reasons (although it may do that as well)' (11).

Scanlon thus, rejects the view that his contractualism is best understood as an account of what makes acts wrong. It should, rather, be understood as an account of wrongness itself. It cannot, however, plausibly be understood as offering an account of the meaning of the word 'wrong', for contractualists and non-contractualists can disagree about what is wrong. Such disagreement would not be possible if 'wrong' meant something different when used by contractualists and non-contractualists (10). So in WWO Scanlon maintains that his contractualist account of wrongness must be understood as a non-analytic account. It tells us what the property of wrongness is, but not what we mean by 'wrong' (12).

In his reply to Mark Timmons and Derek Parfit Scanlon rejects this understanding of his contractualism on the ground that it leads to 'an odd divergence between the concept of moral wrongness and the property of wrongness' (Chapter 7, 137). When a teleological utilitarian, or a divine command theorist says that an action is wrong, and a contractualist denies this, they are disagreeing about the applicability of the concept of wrongness. But if the view that Scanlon expressed in *WWO* is correct, their disagreement would not consist in the fact that one side is affirming that the action has a certain property, and the other denying this. So,

> 'this account describes the two sides as disagreeing about the applicability of the concept of wrongness to the action in question, but not in the properties they are claiming this action to have (438).

To avoid this odd consequence Scanlon has abandoned the view that contractualism provides an account of the property of wrongness. He still rejects the view that his contractualism provides an account of the ground of wrongness. Instead he proposes what he calls 'the ground level description'. 'To claim that an act is wrong is to claim that it violates standards that we have good reason to take very seriously' (Chapter 7, 135). According to the ground level description, Scanlon's contractualism describes in general terms what those standards are, and why we should take them very seriously. I have outlined Scanlon's view about the nature of these important standards. I now turn to his account of why we should take these standards so seriously.

Priority and importance

The special significance of judgements of moral wrongness consists in their having a certain priority and importance. Moral wrongness has priority in the sense that the fact that some act is morally wrong (almost) always defeats other considerations (148). The importance of moral wrongness consists in the fact that failure to see why the fact that's some act is morally wrong gives us a strong reason not to do it is regarded as an especially serious fault (149). The problem of explaining the priority and importance of morality is Scanlon's interpretation of what is often called the problem of moral motivation.

Both priority and importance need to be explained, but such an explanation must avoid Prichard's dilemma (150). According to Prichard's dilemma, either (a) wrongness itself provides a strong reason not to act wrongly, or (b) non-moral considerations provide this reason. The problem with (a) is that it presupposes the reason-giving force of wrongness and so risks triviality. The problem with (b) is that it provides the wrong kind of reason, and so runs the risk of seeming to offer an implausibly external reason for being moral (149–150). An explanation of the normativity of wrongness must, therefore, make reference to considerations that are close enough to morality to avoid irrelevance, but not so close that the explanation is trivial.

There are two general ways of addressing the problem of moral motivation. One may provide either a formal or a substantive account of moral motivation. A formal account avoids appeal to particular ends, e.g., Kant, Habermas. A substantive account, on the other hand, aims to explain the reason-giving force of morality with reference to some substantive form of value, e.g., Christian Aristotelianism or utilitarianism.

Formal accounts have the advantage of making morality inescapable (as requirements of rationality, independent of any substantive good), but fail to provide a satisfactory account of what is wrong with someone who fails to act as they should. Substantive account makes good this deficiency, but must explain why some substantive value take priority over others, and why everyone must recognise this value (151). What is needed, therefore, is

'to explain more clearly how the idea that an act is wrong flows from the idea that there is an objection of a certain kind to people's being allowed to perform such actions, and we need to do this in a way that makes clear how an act's being wrong in the sense described can provide a reason not to do it' (153).

The substantive good to which Scanlon's account appeals is that of an ideal of justifying one's actions to others on grounds that they could not reasonably reject (154). To want to act in ways that could be justified to others is to embrace the value of *mutual recognition*.

"Standing in this relation to others is appealing in itself – worth seeking for its own sake. A moral person will refrain from lying to others, cheating, harming, or exploiting them, 'because these things are wrong'. But for such a person these require-ments are not just formal imperatives; they are aspects of the positive value of a way of living with others" (162).

Mutual recognition involves acting and deliberating in accor-dance with principles that others could not reasonably reject, and the pain of guilt involves a feeling of estrangement from such a valuable relation.

We have reason to give priority to moral reasons when they con-flict with other values because of the importance of the relation of mutual recognition. Scanlon also argues that we should give priority to morality because moral values underpin other, non-moral values. Non-moral values, such as friendship, involve recognising others as separate persons with moral standing – as individuals who are owed justification in their own right (not merely as friends).

"A person who saw only friends as having this sort of status would therefore not have friends in the sense I am describing: their moral standing would be too dependent on the contin-gent fact of his affection. There would ... be something unnerv-ing about a 'friend' who would steal a kidney for you if you needed one. This is not just because you would feel guilty toward the person whose kidney was stolen, but because of what it implies about the 'friend's' view of your right to your own body parts: he wouldn't steal them, but that is only because he happens to like you" (164–5).

Friendship requires not only preferential treatment, but also that we recognise the independent moral standing of our friends, and do not make this recognition conditional on our friendship. So friendship is not a value that is in essential conflict with the value of morality.

Morality sometimes involves seeing some (non-moral) consid-erations as providing no justification to act immorally. Such con-siderations are not regarded as being outweighed by moral reasons. The fact that I would benefit by murdering someone is not a reason to murder that is outweighed by the wrongness of murder. If it were, then if the benefit to me were great enough this self-interested reason would outweigh the opposing moral reason. The fact that I would benefit in this way is no reason at all to commit murder. Morality *excludes* such reasons from consideration (156–7). This important aspect of the priority of morality can be explained in contractualist terms. The excluded considerations are ones that others could reasonably refuse to license us to count as reasons in the relevant circumstances (157).

The importance of morality is explained with reference to the way in which failure to value mutual recognition affects the relations in which we stand to others. Blindness to the reason-giving nature of certain things affects the sort of relations we can enter into with others. If I am blind to art, you cannot discuss such things with me, and we would not be able to enjoy them together. This effect is much more wide-ranging in relation to morality than it is to art, and Scanlon offers a contractualist explanation of its scope.

"This failure makes a more fundamental difference because what is in question is not a shared appreciation of some external value but rather the person's attitude towards us – specifically, a failure to see why the justifiability of his or her actions to us should be of any importance. Moreover, this attitude includes not only us but everyone else as well, since the amoralist does not think that anyone is owed the consideration that morality describes just in virtue of being a person" (p. 159).

Ultimately the special significance of the morality of what we owe to each other is explained with reference to an important and worthwhile relation with others, participation in which will make the agent's own life go better. This explanation of the priority and importance of morality does not, however, aim to ground morality in personal well-being. Mutual recognition does not have value because participation in this relation makes our life go better in various ways. Rather, participation makes our life go better because mutual recognition has value; a value that is close enough to morality to provide a suitable explanation of morality's importance and priority, but not so close that this explanation is empty.

Philip Stratton-Lake
University of Reading
18 December 2003

Bibliography

Kamm, F. (2002). 'Owing, Justifying, and Rejecting'. *Mind*, 111, 300–331

Otsuka, M. (2000). 'Scanlon and the claims of the many versus the one'. *Analysis*, 60.3, 288–293.

Norcross, A. (2002). 'Contractualism and Aggregation'. *Social Theory and Practice*, 28, 303–314.

Raz, J. (1999). *Practical Reasons and Norms*. Oxford: Oxford University Press.

Ridge, M. (2001). 'Saving Scanlon: Contractualism and Agent-Relativity'. *Journal of Political Philosophy*, 2001, 9, 472–481.

Scanlon, T. M. (1998). *What We Owe To Each Other*. Cambridge, Mass.: Harvard University Press.

—— (2002a). 'Replies'. *Social Theory and Practice*, 28, 337–358.

—— (2002b). 'Reasons, Responsibility, and Reliance: Replies to Wallace, Dworkin and Deigh'. *Ethics*, 112, 507–528.

Stratton-Lake, P. (2003a). 'Scanlon's contractualism and the redundancy objection'. *Analysis*, 63.1, 70–76.

—— (2003b). 'Scanlon, permissions and redundancy: Response to McNaughton and Rawling'. *Analysis*, 63.4, 332–337.

Wallace, J. (2002). 'Scanlon's Contractualism'. *Ethics*, 112, 429–470.

2

CONSTRUCTIVISM VS. CONTRACTUALISM

Onora O'Neill

1. The ambitions of constructivisms in ethics

Are Constructivism and Contractualism different, and if so how? Seemingly they are not wholly different, and certainly not incompatible, since some writers have described themselves as both. As a first shot one might suggest that contractualists ground ethical or political justification in *agreement* of some sort, whereas constructivists ground them in some conception of *reason*. This will not provide any neat separation of the two approaches to justification, since agreement may provide a basis for reasons, and reasoning a way of achieving agreement. In opening up these questions a bit further I shall consider some of the moves John Rawls and Tim Scanlon make in talking about their own methods of ethics, and in particular, some of the connections they draw between their *methods* and the *scope* of their accounts of ethical reasoning.

In his early writings Rawls speaks of his work as *contractarian* (others prefer the terms *contractualist* and *contractualism*; I shall use them indifferently), and this may seem appropriate to what he does. He claims to carry 'to a higher level of abstraction the familiar theory of the social contract as found, say, in Locke, Rousseau and Kant'.[1] His theory of justice appears to be grounded in the notion of *agreement* in the Original Position (OP). Yet OP is a rather perverse use of the idea of an agreement or contract, in that the veil of ignorance obscures everything that distinguishes one agent from another. OP seemingly obliterates the very context for any *agreement* or *contract* by eliminating distinctions between persons: it trivialises the notion of agreement by eliminating the possibility of disagreement.

However Rawls's use of OP is neither the sole nor the most convincing basis for thinking of his work as contractarian. He makes a second and deeper use of the notion of agreement in *A Theory*

---

[1]   1 # 3 11; preface viii.

of Justice. This deeper use of the idea of agreement is embedded in the Reflective Equilibrium (RE) that supposedly justifies the choice of OP as a device for generating principles of justice. RE assumes that it makes sense to talk about 'our' considered judgements, which are refined by testing their coherence with proposed principles of justice. Reflective equilibrium, which is the deeper level of Rawls's justification, assumes that 'we' agree on certain considered judgements.

In *A Theory of Justice* Rawls did not yet use the word *constructivism.* But the idea of *construction* is already present in its account of ethical method. Rawls speaks of the principles of justice for which he argues as providing '*constructive criteria*', that is to say procedures for settling moral problems.[2] This rather limited view of constructivism stresses the *practicality* of constructive theories, which provide *criteria* or *procedures* for guiding action. Rawls contrasts constructive positions with 'intuitionism', which he characterises as *impractical* (so *not constructive*) because it prescribes a plurality of unranked principles, so offers no way of settling moral disputes. This early, thin conception of *ethical construction* leads Rawls to classify both Utilitarianism and his own more Kantian position(s) as constructive: both are contrasted with positions in ethics which offer no *constructive criteria*, so are not, or not reliably, practical. Some non-Kantian writers, for example David Gauthier, rightly view their own work as aiming at *constructive criteria* in this thin sense, although their approach is in no way Kantian.[3] They are *constructivists*, but not *Kantian constructivists.* Clearly if we stick with this very minimal understanding of *constructivism*, there will be many forms of constructivism, of which *Kantian constructivisms* will be but one genre.

If this were all that was meant by the term *constructivist*, it would be of limited interest. But most would-be ethical constructivists take a stronger view of constructivism. In particular, they reject or (at least) bracket moral realism. They assign no place or weight to distinctively moral facts or properties, whether natural or nonnatural, that can be *discovered* or *intuited* and do not seek foundations for ethics in such facts. John Rawls stresses his rejection of moral realism in many passages. This one from 'Themes in Kant's Moral Philosophy' is typical. Rawls denies

---

2   *TJ,* 34, 39–40, 49, 52.
3   David Gauthier, *Morals by Agreement* (Oxford: Oxford University Press 1989) and 'Political Contractarianism', *The Journal of Political Philosophy*, 2 (1997), 132–48, in which he explicitly labels his own position *constructivist.*

that first principles, as statements about good reasons, are regarded as true or false in virtue of a moral order of values that is prior to and independent of our conceptions of person and society, and of the public and social role of moral doctrines.[4]

If there was an independent moral order of values, and it could be known, moral realism could be established: in that case constructive approaches to ethics would be redundant.

Ethical constructivisms of the more robust sort reject or bracket moral realism. But they do not embrace those anti-realist positions that give up on the entire project of justification in ethics (e.g. emotivism), or that settle for conceptions of justification too weak to support a robust form of objectivity in ethics (e.g. relativism, communitarianism). Constructivism in ethics is not therefore reducible to any form of conventionalism about ethics. Ethical constructivism, as Rawls came to see it, embodies distinctive and robust claims. It holds that, although realist underpinnings are unobtainable, (some) objective, action-guiding ethical prescriptions can be justified. Can these ambitions be sustained?

2. From contract to construction: Scope and method in Rawls's work

In his earlier work, and in particular in *A Theory of Justice*,[5] Rawls claims that OP is justified by the fact that the principles of justice it would select are in reflective equilibrium with 'our' considered judgements. He apparently sees this approach as providing reasons for action for a loosely specified 'us', perhaps for anybody. It was not easy to see how 'we' are defined, and many readers of the work took it that 'we' included *anybody*, or indeed *everybody*. In fact, a careful reading of *A Theory of Justice* would have revealed that Rawls always set reasoning about justice within the context of a bounded society: 'we' are viewed as fellow members of some closed and bounded society. The scope of Rawls's *Theory of Justice* is restricted. His later work is more explicit in linking his

---

[4]   John Rawls, 'Themes in Kant's Moral Philosophy', (*TKMP*) in John Rawls, *Collected Papers* (Cambridge, Mass.: Harvard University Press, 1989) 497–528; 511.
[5]   John Rawls, *A Theory of Justice* (*TJ*) (Cambridge, Mass: Harvard University Press, 1971).

claims about *scope* – justice is internal to a society – to his view of *constructivist methods* – ethical principles are constructed by reasoning and agreement among fellow citizens within such a society.

In emphasising this link Rawls rejected the better-known link between *scope* and *method* in ethics that underlies communitarian thinking. Since he does not assume social or ethical homogeneity, nor therefore agreement on the good within bounded societies, communitarianism is a non-starter as a basis for an account of justice. For example, in *Political Liberalism* Rawls states that citizens of free societies will adhere to a variety of reasonable comprehensive moral views, that 'pluralism about the good' is unavoidable in free societies.[6] He therefore accepts that neither OP, nor the principles and institutions of justice can be justified as uniquely in Reflective Equilibrium with 'our' considered views: for 'we' may not share such views. Rather OP is to be justified on the basis of a contingent, overlapping consensus among those with varying fundamental views, who may lack a common view of the good. Constructivist methods cannot justify a comprehensive theory of the good.[7]

This more explicit account of normative justification went hand in hand with a more restricted view of the scope of the principles that could be justified. Rawls came to think that justificatory strategies should be fundamentally *political* rather than *metaphysical.* Justice as fairness, he makes explicit in his later writing, may be in reflective equilibrium with *various* comprehensive moral views, but it is justified by the central ideas of a public democratic culture, within which a form of *public reason* may be shared by (perhaps only by) fellow-citizens. This conception of public reason provides a common coin for arguments about justice among fellow-citizens, who need not agree about the good: but it is not a universal currency: 'Those who reject constitutional democracy' he notes '. . . will of course reject the very

---

[6]   John Rawls, *Political Liberalism* (*PL*) (New York, NY: Columbia University Press, 1993). Rawls's first major arguments against comprehensive moral justification date back to *Kantian Constructivism in Moral Theory* (*KC*) in John Rawls, *Collected Papers*, (Harvard University Press, 1980), 303–58. Cf. 'Justice as fairness, as a constructivist view, holds that not all the moral questions we are prompted to ask in everyday life have answers' (*KC* 350).

[7]   See the post-1980 papers in the *Collected Papers*, in particular 'The Idea of an Overlapping Consensus', (*OC*, 1987) 421–48 and 'The Domain of the Political and Overlapping Consensus', (*DPOC*, 1989) 473–496 as well as John Rawls, 'Reply to Habermas', *Journal of Philosophy*, XCII, 1995, 132–79, esp. 143.

idea of public reason'.[8] Here the *scope* and *method* of reasoning about justice are very clearly linked, giving rise to two difficulties. The first difficulty is that Rawls's conception of public reason may seem to rest too much on processes that *happen* to lead to agreement, so robbing whatever is agreed of deeper justification. The second difficulty is that Rawls found it hard to extend his theory of justice across borders. Both problems are by now well known, and I simply note that links between *scope* and *method* play a deep part in Rawls' theory, and say no more.

Nor will I comment on the interesting question whether Rawls's later views of ethical justification are *more* or *less* Kantian than his earlier views. I note only that it is far from clear that Rawls's fundamental strategy of justification is Kantian. Like Kant, Rawls does not appeal to *individual preferences*, or to a notional *hypothetical social contract*, or to an *independent order of moral values*.[9] But unlike Kant, Rawls's basic approach to justification is apparently coherentist. His account of the reasonable (as opposed to the *merely, instrumentally rational*) assigns weight to what happens to be shared among fellow citizens, and his version of public reason assumes the boundaries of some actual public or people. In consequence his account of ethical justification is not universal in scope, and unsurprisingly his conception of justice is not cosmopolitan.

The limits of this form of constructivism are displayed in *Political Liberalism*, whose aim is to 'bring out the bases of the principles of right and justice in practical reason', (*PL* xxx) now conceived of as public *reason* Rawls characterises persons as reasonable when

> they are ready to propose principles and standards as fair terms of co-operation and to abide by them willingly, given the assurance that others will likewise do so. (*PL* 49)

The others who may share a commitment to public reason are fellow-citizens of a democratic society. That is what allows them to 'govern their conduct by a principle from which they and

[8] John Rawls, *The Law of Peoples and the idea of Public Reason Revisited*, Cambridge, Mass.: Harvard University Press, 1999, 32.
[9] Kant uses the notion of a social contract only at a much more specific level of his political philosophy. For chapters and verses see Onora O'Neill, 'Kant and the Social Contract Tradition,' in François Duchesneau, Guy Lafrance et Claude Piché, eds., *Kant Actuel: Hommage à Pierre Laberge* (Montréal: Bellarmin, 2000) 185–200.

others can reason in common' (*PL* 49n): Fellow-citizens are seen as sharing a bounded and closed territory and democracy. So bounded states and democracy are *presupposed* rather than *justified* in Rawls's theory of justice. These features of his position suggest to me that it would have been appropriate for him to continue to speak of his position as *contractualist*: agreement lies at the basis of his account of the reasonable. In 'Justice as Fairness, Political on Metaphysical' he states explicitly that:

> justification is addressed to others who disagree with us, and therefore it must always proceed from some consensus, from premises we and others publicly recognise as true. (*JFPM* 394; cf. *OC* 426)

In the end, I believe, Rawls' theory of justice is more Rousseauian than Kantian, more civic than cosmopolitan, more contractualist than constructivist. Contingent agreement between fellow citizens lies at the basis of his account of public reason, hence of ethical justification, and he could well have continued to speak of his position as *contractarian or contractualist*.

3. Scanlon on desire

In *What We Owe to Each Other* Scanlon speaks of his position as *contractualist* rather than *constructivist*, and immediately comments that 'I will continue to use this name, despite the fact that it has certain disadvantages'. (WWO 5) He distinguishes his form of contractualism from others by 'its conception of the motivational basis of this agreement' (5) and specifically rejects the contractualisms (such as the one proposed by Gauthier) in which the motivation that underlies agreement is self-interest or pursuit of one's own advantage.

However, Scanlon's initial statement of his position may also seem to give weight to a distinctive but contingent type of motivation. The parties to the agreement 'are assumed not merely to be seeking some kind of advantage but also to be moved by the aim of finding principles that others similarly motivated could not reasonably reject' (5). They may not agree on the presuppositions of shared citizenship: but they want to agree on something. Read out of context these claims seem to bring Scanlon's position quite close to Rawls and also (as he notes) to Rousseau. Like them, Scanlon apparently appeals to a distinctive, extra-rational source

of contingently shared motivation, and proposes that ethical conclusions are to be reached by using the principles that *others with
the appropriate motivation* will share. This suggests that Scanlon's
contractualist justifications will fail when motivation is not shared,
and that his reasoning will lack justificatory force when others
(e.g. outsiders or the ill-disposed) happen not to have the relevant motivation. If so, the practical reasoning he endorses will
offer reasons only to others with the appropriate motivation. The
scope of his ethical reasoning will therefore be limited by the fact
that it does not offer reasons to those who don't happen to share
that motivation.

I think Scanlon is less like Rawls than his basic formulation of
contractualism suggests. Although he states that the motivational
basis of ethics is 'a desire to act in a way that can be justified to
others' (7) he insists that it is not *desires* but *reasons* that are fundamental, and that 'the notion of a desire . . . needs to be understood in terms of taking something to be a reason' (7–8). On
Scanlon's account *reason* is fundamentally normative, and its
'motivational' capacity is simply a corollary of this normativity.
(19)

Scanlon sees reason as directed to 'judgement sensitive attitudes'. These include 'attitudes of rational agents such as beliefs,
intentions, hopes, fears . . . admiration, respect, contempt, indig-
nation' (20). 'Judgement sensitive attitudes' are 'complicated sets
of dispositions to act and react in specified ways'. (21) This may
seem to accept a traditional, 'Humean' view of motives or motivation as psychological states, that cause and can in part explain
action.

Yet I suspect that 'judgement sensitive attitudes' cannot be
accurately identified with dispositions to act, because they are
likely to be interlocked in complex ways that undermine any identification with a disposition to act in a certain way. Although we
can formulate a canonical account of, say, an attitude of hostility
towards A, as a disposition *other things being equal* to avoid A or to
act to harm A, as soon as we note that other things are *rarely* equal,
we must also accept that hostility is very often not expressed in
these ways. It is only when we think of 'judgement-sensitive attitudes' in artificial, we might say ideal-typical, isolation that we can
characterise them as 'dispositions to act and react in specified
ways'. As Scanlon points out 'The possibility of overruling and
being overruled is a distinctive characteristic of judgements and
judgement sensitive attitudes'. (24) In context, the way a given

attitude shows, *if at all,* may be very unlike the stereotyped behaviour that *would* express that attitude if other things were equal (whatever exactly that means).

Another way of characterising 'judgement-sensitive attitudes' that brings out some reasons why normative reasoning bears on them rather better, is to note that they are *propositional attitudes.* A focus on the fact that acts and attitudes have propositional *structure and content,* rather than on any motivational *force,* might yield a better grasp of 'judgement-sensitive attitudes'.[10] Judgement-sensitive attitudes are attitudes held by agents at some time; they have propositional structure and content that enable reasoning and justification to bear on them.

And indeed, Scanlon's account of 'judgement-sensitive attitudes' does not treat motives as causally effective states or dispositions of an agent. For example, he writes:

> A rational person who judges there to be sufficient grounds for believing that P normally has that belief and this judgement is normally sufficient explanation for so believing. There is no need to appeal to some further source of motivation such as wanting to believe. (33)

As he sees it, explanations of beliefs or attitudes that *p* can simply appeal to normatively sufficient reasons for believing *that p* or taking an attitude *to p.* Explanation, in this *thin* sense, makes no claims about causal antecedents or motives for holding beliefs or attitudes. Desires and wants are redundant elements in Scanlon's contractualism, and the Humean truism that desires are motivationally efficacious but reasons inert is rejected. (37)

This is not always obvious from the text, since Scanlon also writes: 'it is uncontroversial that desires in this broad sense are capable of moving us to act'. (37) But by *desires in this broad sense* he does not mean states of an agent that would cause congruent action in (whatever) relevant conditions. He means simply 'any pro-attitude toward an action or outcome' (37) – and pro-attitudes are by definition attitudes that favour action of the relevant type. In short, the link between judgement-sensitive attitudes and action is not causal: even under ideal conditions it is

---

[10] This thought is parallel to the thought that in understanding what Kant meant by a *maxim,* we do better to avoid the terms *motive* or *motivation,* and to note simply that a maxim is an agent's practical principle at some time, so has propositional structure and content which enable reasoning and justification to bear on it.

not causal. Rather, anything that moves us is likely to count as a desire in a *thin* or (according to Scanlon) *broad* sense of the term. Desires in the *thin, broad sense* are identified with *whatever* offers reasons for action, rather than with independently knowable states of agents that cause acts of certain types. Scanlon concludes that 'having what is generally called a desire involves a tendency to see something as a reason'. He says a certain amount that fits with accounts of desires as unbidden psychological states, but as I read him, Scanlon parts company with empiricism in the theory of action. Desires as *tendencies to see something as a reason,* or as *directed-attention,* or as *judgement-sensitive attitudes* are not he insists 'unique or independent sources of motivation' (40), and when we do act on a desire 'the motive for this action is the agent's perception of some consideration as a reason, not some additional or independent element of 'desire'. (41) Desires in this *thin, broad* sense do not fit a traditional, thick account of desires as original existences or as causes of action. Equally, desires are not the most revealing of judgement-sensitive attitudes because they set less demanding constraints than some other judgement-sensitive attitudes. A rational agent may desire *p and q,* knowing that *p* is not consistent with *q,* but cannot believe or hope or expect that *p and q,* knowing that *p* is not consistent with *q.*

Yet although Scanlon states bluntly that 'there is no separate problem of motivation' he holds onto the 'familiar label' of *moral motivation,* while warning that it can mislead. I am not sure why he does this. Does he see the issue as a choice between *jettisoning* or alternatively *disempowering* the idea of motivation, i.e. a tactical decision? I am inclined to think that having made so decisive a move in his views of *desire* and *motivation,* it might have been simpler if he had ceded both terms to those who claim that desires and motives are causes of action, that must be identified for explanation and may be invoked for justification of action. However, his approach is to hold on to the terms *desire* and *motivation,* while rejecting the view that 'desires are not conclusions of practical reasoning but starting points for it' (45) and contending that 'desires almost never provide reasons in the way described in the standard desire model' (43) and concluding that practical reasoning is not a matter of balancing competing desires on the basis of their "strength" (54) and that 'when a rational person recognises something as a reason we do not need a further explanation of how he or she could be moved to act" (154).

4. Scanlon's contractualism: Scope and method

Where does Scanlon end up having pushed certain common understandings of *desire* and *motivation* to the periphery of his account to justification? Where in particular does it lead his account of practical reasoning? And is the position to which he is led more contractualist (based on agreement) or more constructivist (practical, anti-realist, objectivist)?

Scanlon starts his account of (practical) reason with the minimal thought that 'a reason is a consideration that counts in favour of some judgement-sensitive attitude'. (67) The weak conception of a reason for action *for an individual*, which Scanlon takes as primitive, embodies only a slender view of differences between good and bad reasons for action. Yet an individual's reasons for action must presumably be coherent and intelligible, and should not reflect unwarranted beliefs, although they may be idiosyncratic, peculiar or selfish. Reasons for action in this minimal sense are no more than pro-attitudes directed towards action falling under some description. I find it surprising that Scanlon does not say more about rational constraints on individual reasons for action.

A stronger account of differences between good and bad reasons for action is needed if agents are to seek to justify ways of action to one another. Scanlon characterises contractualism as the claim that an act is wrong if 'its performance would be disallowed by any set of principles for the reasonable regulation of behavior that "no one could reasonably reject as a basis for unforced general agreement."'[11] The focus on principles that 'no one could reasonably reject as a basis for unforced general agreement' looks very like Rawls's position. Yet it cannot be close to Rawls's position because Scanlon does not help himself even to a minimal 'political' account of the basis of antecedent *agreement* or *co-ordination* or *shared outlook*, such as those fellow citizenship in a democratic polity provide in Rawls's theory of justice. Hence he cannot adopt Rawls's account of justifying principles to one another. Yet since his account of motivation does not, as I have argued, do any independent work he also cannot base justification on it. So what does the work of distinguishing

[11] In a second formulation of contractualism, motivation seemingly gets no look in: 'the ideal to which contractualism appeals . . . is that of being able to justify your action'. (154)

good from bad reasons for action beyond individual reasons for action?

Scanlon's account of practical reasoning bears on *processes* (246), on possible exchanges of considerations between agents, that might be used to justify, but he does not set it out as a systematic or formal account of the structure of practical reasoning. He draws on the idea of a plurality of agents who exchange what they take to be reasons, so have to put forward to others 'judgement sensitive attitudes' that (they take it) those others can follow and appreciate. He rejects utilitarian contractualism, in which agents agree that desire satisfaction provides canonical reasons for action. He rejects welfare contractualism in which they agree that well being provides a canonical reason for action; given his views on desires as reasons for action he could hardly do otherwise. He views the substance of the individual reasons for action that agents may appeal to in trying to justify action to one another as heterogeneous. E.g. some reasons that are offered may refer to the benefits or burdens of accepting certain proposals; others to the fairness or unfairness of doing so. Since Scanlon has taken reasons as *primitive*, it is consistent that he not offer any definitive analysis of the necessary and sufficient conditions for anything offered to count as a reason.

Moral justification arises from a process of offering and receiving, accepting and rejecting purported reasons for action. The work is done simply by the consideration that justification has to reach others to whom we seek to justify action or proposals. So we have to have some connection to those others, and specifically to recognise them as others; but we need not share their beliefs or attitudes. To seek to justify is to make moves that others, within the scope of those whom we recognise, might either accept or reject.

The scope of justification can vary for different sorts of practical reasoning. Justifying action to a friend 'involves recognising the friend as a separate person with moral standing – as someone to whom justification is owed in his or her own right.' (164 cf. 168) But moral justification reaches wider. It addresses the question 'What general principles of action could we all will?' (171) At this – very Kantian – juncture, Scanlon asserts 'the idea of justifiability to others and the idea of respecting their value cease to be distinct'. (171) The point of convergence in the process of exchanging reasons – of mutual justification – must be 'an accept-

able system of general principles of action'. The process of justification takes account of justifications anyone could raise while
recognising the force of other similar objections. (171) One characterisation of Scanlonian contractualism would be that it enjoins
each not to regard himself or herself as an exception, and so to
accept only principles that could coherently be proposed to (all)
others. The constraints of contractualism go beyond the coherence requirements that bear on individual and local attempts at
mutual justification. They can also take account of the thought
that certain principles – for example, principles of justice – are
justified only if they can be principles for all. The inclusive scope
of moral principles is the basis of justification, or (putting it the
other way round) the inadequacy of some putative reasons is
that they cannot offer reasons, and is the basis for rejecting
them as morally unacceptable. Contractualism 'locates the source
of the reason giving force of judgements of right and wrong in
the importance of standing in a certain relation to others',
(177–8) and so 'our relation to these beings gives us reason to
accept the requirement that our actions should be justifiable to
them'. (185).

Is *contractualism* the best label for this position? The position
claims that moral justification is directed to an indefinitely large
circle, so cannot presuppose antecedent agreement but only the
recognition that all others are part of the audience for justification. So it seems that agreement is *not* the basis of moral reasoning. Rather agreement can (but need not) be an outcome of
actual processes of attempted justification. Justified principles are
to be such that they cannot be reasonably rejected by any within
the scope of those who recognise one another. Agents who are
committed to the project of justification will winnow the principles with which they start, setting aside as inadequate for certain
purposes any that clearly cannot be accepted by certain others.
This initial move – we may call it the Kantian move – will pick out
principles that for formal reasons cannot be principles for all, as
well as principles that cannot be principles for more restricted
circles.

If Scanlon's account of practical reason is best read along
these lines, his work might be viewed as more constructivist
than contractualist, more Kantian than Rousseauian, and more
constructivist than Rawls's constructivism. Paradoxically Rawls
who characterises his work as *constructivist* might reasonably be
viewed as a *contractualist*; and Scanlon who terms himself a

contractualist makes no basic use of the notion of agreement, and might well be called a *constructivist.*

References

Gauthier, David (1997). 'Political Contractarianism', *The Journal of Political Philosophy*, 2, 132–48.

—— (1989). *Morals by Agreement* (Oxford: Oxford University Press).

O'Neill, Onora (2000). 'Kant and the Social Contract Tradition', in François Duchesneau, Guy Lafrance et Claude Piché (eds), *Kant Actuel: Hommage à Pierre Laberge* (Bellarmin, Montréal), 185–200.

Rawls, John (1971). *Theory of Justice* (Cambridge, Mass: Harvard University Press).

—— (1980). 'Kantian Constructivism in Moral Theory', in *Collected Papers* (Harvard University Press), 303–58.

—— (1987). 'The Idea of an Overlapping Consensus', in *Collected Papers* (Harvard University Press), 421–48.

—— (1989). 'Themes in Kant's Moral Philosophy', in John Rawls, *Collected Papers* (Harvard University Press), 497–528.

—— (1989). 'The Domain of the Political and Overlapping Consensus', in *Collected Papers* (Harvard University Press), 473–96.

—— (1993). *Political Liberalism* (New York, NY: Columbia University Press).

—— (1995). 'Reply to Habermas', *Journal of Philosophy*, XCII, 132–79.

Scanlon, T. M. (1998). *What We Owe To Each Other* (Cambridge, Mass: Harvard University Press).

3

SCANLON ON WELL-BEING

Jonathan Wolff

Jeremy Bentham opens Introduction to the *Principles of Morals and Legislation* with the remark:

> Nature has placed mankind under the governance of two sovereign masters, *pain* and *pleasure*. It is for them alone to point out what we ought to do, as well as to determine what we shall do. On the one hand the standard of right and wrong, on the other the chain of causes and effects are fastened to their throne. They govern us in all we do, in all we say, in all we think: every effort to throw off our subjection, will serve but to demonstrate and confirm it. In words a man may pretend to abjure their empire: but in reality he will remain subject to it all the while. The principle of utility recognizes this subjection, and assumes it for the foundation of that system, the object of which is to rear the fabric of felicity by the hands of reason and law. Systems which attempt to question it deal in sounds instead of sense, in caprice instead of reason, in darkness instead of light. (Bentham 1970, p. 11)

The idea that some good or value, such as pleasure and the avoidance of pain, can play such a dual role of motivation and justification sustains utilitarianism and other forms of consequentialism. Without a clear notion of the good utilitarianism cannot get started. With it, it becomes hard to resist the thought that the more of it the better. Critics of utilitarianism are forced on the defensive; perhaps the assumed notion of the good is too narrow – there is more to life than pleasure and the avoidance of pain. Or perhaps we should temper quantity with distribution.

In his earlier paper 'Contractualism and Utilitarianism' Scanlon famously remarked

> What a successful alternative to utilitarianism must do, first and foremost, is to sap this source of strength by providing a clear account of the foundations of non-utilitarian moral reasoning. (Scanlon 1982, p. 103)

This thought was admiringly endorsed by Philippa Foot, who suggested that we concede too much to utilitarianism from the start by allowing that one state of affairs might, all things considered, be better than another (Foot 1985). Now although we might be sympathetic to her strategy of argument, whether she has come up with the right diagnosis of our false seduction by utilitarianism is at least arguable. And indeed, although he does not explicitly frame it as such, we might read Scanlon's chapter on well-being as an alternative attempt to cut utilitarianism off at the knees, by arguing that there is no notion capable of playing the role that utilitarianism needs. On this reading the point is not merely to provide an alternative source of moral reasoning, but to argue that utilitarianism is not entitled to its own source.

Few in the contemporary utilitarian tradition will want to follow Bentham's claim that we are physically determined to seek pleasure and avoid pain. But a doubly amended substitute claim about rationality and well-being seems more plausible: there is a notion of well-being such that it is rational to wish to pursue it to the extent that one can. Well-being is of value, and as such is to be promoted. Once this much is conceded, consequentialism has its foothold, and will be very hard to dislodge. There may be no way of getting from here to a view with a different structure, and this, I think, is why it is thought so important to diverge from utilitarianism's path at this early stage.

But what are the alternatives? It has become customary to divide approaches to moral theory into three types; broadly speaking Kantian, Consequentialist and Aristotelian. Now the clarity and usefulness of this distinction has often been questioned, and, as so often is the case in philosophy, the views themselves only receive crystal clear characterisation in the hands of their opponents as a preface to refutation. The defence will then take a predictable form: that the theory is not committed to whatever it is that led to the criticism.

Despite this, it seems to me that there is a valuable lesson to be learnt from the division of the subject into these broad traditions. Ultimately what seems to me to distinguish them is their account of what is morally fundamental to human beings. Kantian theories emphasise that human beings have reason and a will, and are capable of agreeing and disagreeing with proposals about what should happen to them. Consequentialist theories, at least in classical form, start with the idea that human beings are capable of pleasure and pain, and this should be paramount in how we should treat each other. Aristotelian theories take as primitive the idea that human beings have a good, and thus are capable of flourishing or withering. If we accept this basis of the division then the character of a moral theory is best appreciated through an investigation of which of these features it takes to be fundamental and which derivative. So, for example, the fact that one theory can use a notion from another tradition is of little fundamental significance. Both Kantians and Utilitarians have pointed out, for example, that they can make use of the notion of human flourishing. But the question is whether it has fundamental or derivative status within the theory.[1]

How the notion of well-being fits into this picture is a good question. On the face of it, it is of wider scope than the idea of pleasure, but less organic than the notion of an individual good. So it straddles the consequentialist/Aristotelian divide. This is not an objection either to my classification or to the idea of well-being. Any theory has to come to an understanding of the importance of the central three notions, and producing such a mid-range concept is one way of arbitrating between two of them, and trying to get the best out of two distinct traditions of thought.

Scanlon, as a contractualist, would obviously give the idea of agreement central place, and many comments amply confirm this (see, e.g. Scanlon 1998, p. 169). This does not mean, however, that he should attempt to designate other notions as irrelevant. Rather, they may find a place in his theory without determining the overall nature or structure of that theory. And this is, I think, exactly his attitude towards the idea of well-being. Consequentialist theories assume that well-being is a 'master value', things are good or valuable only in so far as they contribute to well-being. However, he argues, it is not a master-value. So consequentialism is not a plausible account of our morality.

As Scanlon presents matters, if well-being is a master value, so that any other thing we value is valued only as a means to well-being, three further claims are typically also maintained (although whether they strictly follow is another question, which we will look at later). The three claims are:

---

[1]   It is worth comparing this account with Scanlon's somewhat different list of the possible bases of moral concern (1998, p. 179).

a) It serves as an important basis for the decisions of a single rational individual, at least for those decisions in which he or she alone is concerned.
b) It is what a concerned benefactor, such as a friend or parent, has reason to promote.
c) It is the basis on which an individual's interests are taken into account in moral argument. (Scanlon 1998, p. 108)

A further assumption is that well-being is capable of quantitative comparisons, both within a single individual and, at least in some cases, across individuals, and finally that it can clearly be distinguished from other concepts in the sense of having clear boundaries.

As his subsequent discussion makes clearer Scanlon's last category really splits into two: first the resolution of private moral disputes and problems, where one person's interests come into conflict with another; the other in political decision making where the distribution of benefits and burdens needs to be thought through on a public, social, level. Thus we have four separate contexts in which issues of well-being may arise.

For those with a love of system, it would be very appealing to think that a single notion of well-being could undergird all these areas. Even if this does not give us answers to all questions it at least gives us a way of approaching them all, and to see the systematic relations and connections between levels. But if Scanlon is right, there is no notion of well-being that can play all of these roles.

What, then, is Scanlon's objection? Even before looking at the details of his argument we might conjecture that the general point is likely to fall under one or more of these heads:

a) We simply cannot find anything that fills this brief.
b) There is a principled reason why we will never find such a conception of well-being.
c) Whether or not we can define such a thing, we have no need for it.

However, the position is more complicated in that Scanlon, as noted, does not want to abandon the idea of well-being altogether. He does accept that we can make sense of a broad notion of well-being. Rather, as we saw, his point is that it is a not a master-value, and his position is well summarized in a footnote (Scanlon 1998, p. 395 n 23)

[W]ell-being is not a master value: the value of other things does not always derive from the fact that they make individuals' lives better. But if these things are valuable, then recognizing them does contribute to the quality of people's lives. From an individual's point of view what is primary in most cases is the (impersonal) value of these aims and pursuits. In determining what we owe to each other, however, what matters is the contribution that these values make to individual lives.

The integrated view says: my life goes well for me if I can advance my own well-being to the maximum extent, but morality can require limits to my well-being, in order to advance the well-being of others. This picture apparently assumes a match-up between individual motivation and what we might think of as 'morally basic data': the same thing that I rationally pursue in my life functions as input into moral calculation. Essentially, I think, Scanlon has two main arguments against this. The first is that this gives a false picture of individual motivation:

> We do have a rough, intuitive idea of individual well-being, and we can make rough comparative judgements about what makes a life go better and worse from the point of view of the person who lives it. But this concept of well-being has surprisingly little role to play in the thinking of the rational individual whose life is in question. (p. 109)

The second objection is that the notion of well-being that is used in moral contexts is not morally basic. It will typically be a normative notion in some way: moralised or cleansed. (p. 110)

We will examine these arguments shortly. But, as always, we must raise a question of the ambition of the arguments. Is Scanlon's task simply to give us what he takes to be the true picture, or is it to give arguments that should rationally compel the abandonment of the master-value position? It seems to me that his aim is somewhere in the middle: not so much to convert the notoriously unconvertible, but to put forward considerations that will determine the intellect of those who have no entrenched position to defend. Yet to examine the strength of Scanlon's position it is worth seeing how the master-value theorist might respond.

Let us start by examining the question of what would really be shown if it turned out that we do need to appeal to a differ-

ent conception of well-being in each of the contexts now identified: individual rationality; benefaction; morality; and political
morality. Scanlon appears to assume that this is an important
stage in the demonstration that well-being is not a master value.
However, is that so? Could it not just be that different contexts
create different pressures independent of the notion of well-
being? Consider one of Scanlon's own examples, from his early
paper 'Preference and Urgency'

> The fact that someone would be prepared to forego a decent
> diet in order to build a monument to his god does not mean
> that his claim on others for aid in his project has the same
> strength as a claim for aid in obtaining enough to eat (even
> assuming that the sacrifices required of others would be the
> same) (Scanlon 1975, pp. 659–60).

Clearly in this case the individual in question will evaluate his own
situation from the standpoint of how well he is able to meet his
religious obligations, and, for the sake of the argument, let us say
that this would advance his well-being (although we have to
concede that this does not seem to get things quite right). From
the standpoint of the community, however, the question is how
well he is fed. What explains this mismatch in the terms used to
evaluate his situation?

There could be various explanations, but the immediate question is whether any are consistent with the idea that well-being is
a master value. It seems that there is little difficulty here. It could
be argued that the reason why we don't use an individual's own
notion of well-being in political or public contexts is two-fold.
First, we rarely have fine-grained information, and so need something analogous to what Scanlon calls generic reasons. Second,
we need something for which there can be an adequate process
of public accounting. So for both these reasons we need a cruder,
simplified political account of well-being. However we do this for
indirect consequentialist reasons; this will be the best way to gen-
erate the greatest well-being, even though it does not work in
every particular case.

Now I don't offer this as the correct explanation. However it
does show that there could be reasons for context-dependence in
our accounts of well-being which are consistent nevertheless with
the idea of well-being as a master-value. Still, it may be said that

this type of explanation is not available in the case of context shifts from individual rationality to third-party benefaction. There is no bar to gaining fine-grained information, and public accountability is not relevant. However, we may still argue that different needs apply. For example, one of the principles of gift-giving is to buy people things that they would not have bought for themselves. Another example is that we shouldn't meddle or interfere too much in other people's lives; we should let them find their own way. So only in very serious cases should we try to divert people on to the true path of well-being. This, I think, is behind the US drink driving campaign slogan: 'friends don't let friends drive drunk': the issue is of such seriousness that paternalism is acceptable, even required. Interestingly this is a trope that has been picked up very widely in the US: so you now see advertisements urging that 'friends don't let friends eat frozen fish', or bizarrely 'buy particle board'. Indeed further researches revealed that, somewhat predictably, friends don't let friends use AOL, buy PC's, drink Starbucks or vote Republican. More interestingly, they don't let friends cheerlead, die without Jesus, play trombone, make their own beer, or, my particular favourite, make Power Point presentations.

The serious point, of course, is that we feel we may interfere only in cases where potentially great harm may be suffered. In lesser cases we should perhaps give gentle advice, but stand back and watch mistakes being made. Why so? Perhaps because autonomy is part of well-being or that people will get most well-being from a life where they have learnt from their own mistakes. Again this is a context shift that does not defeat the idea that well-being is a master value.

Now Scanlon could concede all I have said, I think, but argue that nothing so far address his main arguments, the first of which is that the notion of well-being plays little role in individual motivation in any case. So let us now turn to this issue.

This first argument is based on some observations about the phenomenology of action. The modified Benthamite position assumes that it is rational to be motivated by desires to advance our own well-being. Scanlon disputes this on two grounds. First: 'Insofar as "having a desire" is understood as a state which is distinct from "seeing something as a reason," it plays almost no role in the justification and explanation of action.' (Scanlon 1998, p. 18) Second, and more immediately relevant, is the claim that we tend to act not to advance personal well-being but for the sake of the (impersonal) value of our aims and pursuits.

Broadly, then, the picture is that typically I act not because I desire to increase my well-being, but because I judge that what I am doing is worthwhile independently of my attempt to achieve it. Now I have to admit that there is something pleasantly high-minded about this, although Bentham, of course, would claim that it is an intellectualist delusion. However, perhaps action is diverse in nature, and we might want to look at many cases before attempting to say what is generally, typically or never the case.

Consider the following examples of what may be called actions:

1. The drinking of a glass of wine with lunch.
2. Staying on vacation an extra day rather than attending a departmental meeting.
3. Joining an exercise class.
4. Buying a particular model of new car.
5. Enrolling for graduate work in Philosophy.

These vary, broadly, in terms of their significance for one's overall life, although different people would place them in a different order, no doubt. Now I want to leave to one side whether they would typically be the consequence of reason or desire, and I will assume that Scanlon is correct about the role of reason in action and motivation. The question is how would an individual's own sense of their own well-being typically function in the train of deliberation leading to the action. Let us consider three people: one of whom claims to do each of these things because it will bring them pleasure; the second because it will advance their well-being; and the third who claims to do all these things for their impersonal value.

In their deliberations, what questions would they have asked themselves? The first is straightforward: 'what would bring me most pleasure'? The second might say 'what would increase my well-being to the greatest degree?'; or 'what would make my life go best?', and the last must, presumably, ask, 'what is there most reason to do'?

Can we imagine these people: the pleasure seeker, the well-being seeker and the impersonal reasoner? The pleasure seeker seems a clear enough case. He or she might seem rather shallow, and probably not terribly reliable as a friend or colleague, but nevertheless rather admirable, someone it might be good to be more like, at least in certain cases. Michael Stocker has the example of a good departmental citizen who, as a one off, decides not to go to a departmental meeting so as not to forsake the sheer pleasure of another day at the beach (Stocker and Hegeman 1996).

Turning to the next candidate, as Scanlon himself notes, it is hard to characterise the well-being seeker in a plausible way. The question 'what would give me greatest well-being?' is hard to understand, as distinct from the question 'what would give me the greatest sense of well-being?', where one might think of the highs claimed to be experienced by those who exercise furiously, or in the song 'Parklife' by Blur, where feeding the sparrows and pigeons is said to give 'me a sense of enormous well-being'. But a sense of well-being is distinct from well-being. The question: 'What would make my life go best?' is, I think easier to comprehend, but perhaps best not said out loud as it seems somewhat unpleasantly self-obsessed; to imply that one's life has such importance that it should be given special consideration by others as well as oneself. But the idea that one decision rather than another would make one's life go better is nevertheless often hard to comprehend, at least in certain cases, unless there is specification of much more context. It is not merely that we don't know how to answer; it may sometimes not even be clear what exactly is being asked.

Can we imagine the impersonal value seeker, who acts because of the impersonal value of what he or she does? Stanley Fish might argue that this is an excellent sociological observation of the nature of the reasoning of the typical College Professor who ought to 'lighten up a little'. In 'The Unbearable Ugliness of Volvos' he asked why in the 1970s so many US College Professors gave up driving ugly Volkswagens and started driving Volvos when there were plenty of American cars that were more fun to drive, cheaper to buy and run, and just as safe, even though these other manufacturers had not managed to appropriate the idea of safety in the masterful way that Volvo has done. His hypothesis is that professors – unlike other citizens – will rarely if ever do anything for the pleasure it brings (in fact they often seem to prefer misery and disappointment). They always need another, impersonal, reason to rationalise their action (Fish 1994). This, if true, would make a philosopher's introspection a poor basis for a general philosophy of action. In sum, what Scanlon sees as the correct account of action, Fish sees as a sort of character defect.

Now, of course, this is a caricature. On Scanlon's view impersonal value is one good reason for action, but not the only. The value-seeker need not also be a pleasure-denier. More likely such a person would suppose that there are times when considerations of pleasure are not decisive, and Fish's complaint is only that college professors deny themselves pleasure too often. Scanlon need not deny that we drink wine at lunch and stay at the beach for pleasure, join the gym for the sake of our well-being, take up philosophy because of the impersonal value, and buy a particular model of car for whatever reason seems to us most salient in the circumstances.

It should be conceded to Scanlon that it is rare for people to act with the explicit aim, or under the description, of advancing their well-being. Perhaps people will say this only in the case of physical or mental health, although interestingly Scanlon treats health in itself, as distinct from the experience of health, as a marginal component of well-being. Yet from this it doesn't follow that we cannot identify rational action with action that advances an individual's well-being. That is, for all the argument given so far, rational action may be action that as a matter of fact advances one's well-being, whatever its motivation.

Indeed, Scanlon himself gives a plausible enough account of the nature of well-being, in which first, certain experiences, especially enjoyment and satisfaction; second, success in pursuit of rational aims; and third friendship, other personal relations and achievement of excellence are all contributors to an individual's well-being (Scanlon 1998, pp. 124–5).

It is typical of Scanlon's method and temperament not to raise and attempt to answer the question of what these things have in common, beyond all being ways in which an individual's life can go better. We should, of course, understand these items as being components of well-being, rather than being its causes, for that would require us to say in other terms what well-being is; i.e. it would appear to demand the unifying account that Scanlon does not accept.

So, to return to the main thread, why should we not simply conclude that Scanlon has set the standard for what counts as taking well-being as a master value too high? Perhaps what is important is not that people deliberately act in order to advance their well-being, but, rather insofar as they act rationally they do in fact advance their well-being, even if this is not the ocurrent motivation from which they acted.

At this point we may begin to lose grip on the question of what is at stake in the debate about whether well-being is a master-value, and so may be unsure whether substituting this question is a fair move. But in any case Scanlon has a more direct answer. This new proposal rests on the assumption that action that does not (or perhaps could not) advance one's well-being is irrational. But there are two things wrong with this. First, why should it not be the case that acting for the sake of others is rational? Second, to maintain this strategy we need a very clear boundary between those things that advance my well-being and those things that do not. But, Scanlon claims, there is no such clear boundary. So, if he is right, this is no way to make progress.

In sum, then, Scanlon seems to have made this stage of his argument very plausible. It is rare for people to act with the explicit aim of advancing their well-being. Now although there are various ways of advancing one's well-being, and often people's action will have this effect, or be directed towards it in some sense, this just does not give any clear guidance as to what is to count as rational and irrational action.

Finally we turn to the second argument; that the notion of well-being used in moral arguments is already morally cleansed, and thus cannot be the basis or fundamental starting point of a moral view. This does, I think, raise a very important issue. Suppose we identify well-being with preference satisfaction. Now, from the point of view of, say, utilitarian theory which preferences should be entered into the utilitarian calculus? Intuitively we should say 'all of them' but this then raises the spectre of various classes of preferences that may be suspect. There are those, for example, that rest on false belief or faulty reasoning. There are those that are 'nosy' in that they concern what should happen to others, and even how political society should be arranged. Should we take into account, for example, the deontologist's dissatisfaction that preference utilitarianism has been adopted? Finally there are those that are not only nosy, but sadistic: preferences for the preferences of others to be frustrated.

Here the utilitarian faces a very well-known dilemma. Either everything goes into the calculation, and we risk highly counter-intuitive outcomes from the decision mechanism, or we start filtering or adjusting preferences, in which case it appears that preference satisfaction theory loses its clarity and furthermore is no longer morally basic. (Note that this is not how Scanlon himself sets out the dilemma.[2]) Now it seems to me that there is an important difference between filtering out preferences because they are ill-informed and filtering out preferences because they are anti-social. Once the second form of filtering is proposed I think it is clear that Scanlon's case is made; there is a level of morality through which we adjust preferences. I don't think it is possible here to wriggle out on the basis of some indirect consequentialist calculation, for the question here is what goes into the very first calculation. This is different from over-ruling anti-social preferences on the basis of a calculation. So the consistent defender of well-being as a master value owes an explanation of why preference satisfaction from one source adds to well-being, but preference satisfaction from another source does not, and it is hard to see how this is going to be done.

So the best attempt to sustain the master value thesis would be to say that all preferences are to be included unless they are defective as preferences, in the sense of being ill-formed or ill-informed. Assuming the theorist can overcome doubts raised by Scanlon about the coherence of this theory, this pushes us back to the first horn of the dilemma: will there not be counter-intuitive results? However it is hardly news for the utilitarian that those who believe in other theories think it leads to counter-intuitive consequences, and there are plenty of strategies for trying to deal with this.

So considering this part of the argument, it seems open to Scanlon's opponent to say that he or she is unimpressed with the idea that morality must take a notion of well-being that is already morally cleansed. There is no such compulsion, for it is possible to state a preference satisfaction theory of well-being that does not have this requirement.

Is this defence adequate? We should return to the question of Scanlon's ambition. I suggested that he does not set out to refute those who believe that well-being is a master value. And I do believe that they can retreat to a consistent position, which has the following elements:

1. An individual's well-being is a matter of the satisfaction of their informed preferences. (This theory will meet

---

[2]   Scanlon suggests that if we take unfiltered preferences we run the risk of including preferences for things that do not advance well-being. But this, it seems to me, will be resisted on the grounds that it begs the question against the preference theory of well-being.

Scanlon's objection that there is no clear boundary between
well-being and other reasons for action.)

2. Although people often do not act with the explicit aim of
   advancing their well-being so understood, rational action
   nevertheless is action which does, in fact, do this.
3. There are various reasons why in political contexts and cases
   of benefaction we use other notions of well-being, but none
   of this defeats the point that well-being is the satisfaction of
   informed desire.
4. Morality starts from the notion of well-being as satisfaction
   of informed preferences.

Against this Scanlon has his own claims:

1. We have a rough notion of well-being, which includes
   certain experiences, success in rational aims and other
   things too, and there is no unique place for preference
   satisfaction.
2. There are numerous forms of rational action, including
   in some cases acting in ways that will not advance your
   well-being.
3. The fact that we use different notions of well-being in different contexts strongly suggests that well-being is not a
   master-value.
4. Morality does take issues of well-being very seriously, but this
   is only one of a number of factors that need to be taken into
   account in many moral decisions.

So we have a choice. One view can be set out on a postcard, and
if true it provides a unified approach to prudence and morality,
giving clear guidance on every issue. The other view perhaps can
never be set out completely, and provides many small insights but
few if any definitive answers. It is no surprise that the former has
seemed so appealing. But as Scanlon shows, the weight of reason
favours the latter beyond any reasonable doubt.

References

Bentham, Jeremy. (1970). *An Introduction to the Principles of Morals and Legislation*, ed J. H.
  Burns and H. L. A. Hart (London: Athlone Press).
Fish, S. (1994). 'The Unbearable Ugliness of Volvos', in S. Fish, *There's No Such Thing as
  Free Speech* (New York: Oxford University Press).
Foot, P. (1985). 'Utilitarianism and the Virtues', *Mind*, 94, 196–209.
Scanlon, T. M. (1975). 'Preference and Urgency', *Journal of Philosophy*, 72, 655–69.

—— (1982). 'Contractualism and Utilitarianism' in Sen & Williams (eds.), *Utilitarianism and Beyond* (Cambridge: Cambridge University Press) 103–28.

—— (1998). *What We Owe to Each Other* (Cambridge, Mass.: Harvard University Press).

Stocker, M. and Hegeman, E. (1996). *Valuing Emotions* (Cambridge: Cambridge University Press).

4

NUMBERS, WITH AND WITHOUT CONTRACTUALISM

Joseph Raz[1]

Most people find it irritatingly childish to wonder whether there is anything wrong if a lifeguard who can save several people drowning to his right lets them drown in order to save one person drowning on his left, even though saving the several would have been as easy as, and no more risky than saving the one, and he knew that, and knew that he could not save them all, and that he has no special obligation to any of them. Surely, we say, numbers matter. Surely the lifeguard would be wrong not to attempt to save as many as he can.

In exploring the general features of practical reason such cases are challenging. The more obvious the answer the more difficult it is to find non-question-begging reasons for it. Besides not everyone shares the common certitude. Some feel that it is up to the lifeguard, or at least would be up to him if his employment does not impose any special obligations, for example an obligation to save as many people as he can. We will ignore such complications, assuming only that the rescuer has a moral reason to save at least one of the drowning, and that there is no reason to favour or disfavour any of them.

I will take the fundamental practical concept to be that of a reason for action, i.e. of a consideration which makes the action eligible such that if it is performed for that reason it is, other things being equal, an intelligible action (it makes sense to the agent and to others who know of its circumstances) and a rational, justified action, one which is not flawed. If, in other words, the action is irrational or unjustified this is because of other factors which negate or defeat the factors which are reasons for it.[2] I will

---

[1] I am grateful to Véronique Munoz-Dardé, Ulrike Heuer, Timothy Macklem, Penelope Bulloch, Rahul Kumar and Andrew Reisner for helpful comments.
[2] See the account of reasons in *Engaging Reason*. Note that even irrational action is intelligible if done for a reason, and that even unjustified action can be rational if the agent is not culpable for flouting reason. An action is not flawed if it conforms with an undefeated reason. Needless to say this is a somewhat stipulative use of the term. Actions can be open to criticism in other ways.

assume that reasons consist in the fact that actions possess certain evaluative properties making them worth performing, etc. or bad, etc. The reason for an action not yet performed is that it will have the relevant evaluative property if performed. Most of the time our discourse is more flexible and we refer as reasons to facts or states of diverse kinds which are variously connected with the possession of a suitable evaluative property by the action in view. Context disambiguates the connection, and helps in identifying the evaluative property meant.

As mentioned I will consider only reasons for action failure to conform or to try to conform with which is, other things being equal, a flaw, a fault, rendering one's conduct wrong, imprudent, unwise, foolish, or marred by some other defect. My discussion is neutral on whether all reasons are of this kind. Failure to conform with some reasons is, other things being equal, a moral fault, or it renders the action morally wrong (whether or not the agent is blameworthy for it). Some reasons amount to, or establish duties. My discussion will include, but will not be confined to such reasons.

The problem to be discussed here should not be confused with another: if one is morally entitled to refrain from doing some good, but chooses to do it, is one then at fault if one does not do as much good (of that kind) as one can on that occasion? At least sometimes the answer seems to be that if one ventures to do some good, one has to do the best one can. Imagine a situation where though it would have been perfectly all right to stay on shore, you set out in your boat to save a drowning person. Your action may even be foolhardy. But you venture out, and given that you do, can you really pass by and leave another drowning person in the water, if picking him up will not increase the risk to yourself or to the other person you save, and there are no other reasons against saving him? You are already running the risk, or incurring the costs avoidance of which would have justified your forbearing from any rescue attempt. They can no longer justify not saving all those you can with no extra risk and cost. Needless to say this argument presupposes, among much else, the answer to the question to be here considered, namely that if you have a 'fault-making' reason to save some, you have a 'fault-making' reason to save the many rather than the few, other things being equal.

One difficulty with that answer is that it seems to conflict with other views which many find equally obvious. One may not kill a person to use his kidneys to save two who would otherwise die, even though, arguably, it is permissible for a person to choose death in order to donate his kidneys. One need not have two children rather than stop at one, even though, arguably, one may have two for the reason that having a second child will likely bring into being a person who will have a fulfilling life. If so why not save the few, even if one may save the many? The question why do numbers count among the drowning is important to an understanding of why, when, and how they do in general.

An obvious line to explore is that there are reasons of various kinds, and that numbers count within kinds but not across kinds (i.e. not when the reasons involved are of different kinds). That is, e.g., the view taken by Scanlon. I will examine his Contractualist argument for it below. But first, do numbers count at all?

1. Degrees of compliance

If numbers count it must be for reasons independent of Scanlon's Contractualism.[3] His Contractualism is not a general theory of practical reason, but an account of a special category of reasons, those arising out of what we owe each other. Scanlon identifies them with wrong-making reasons. The cogency of his argument does not depend on this identification, and I will not comment on it. It suggests, however, that Scanlon's Contractualism presupposes not only a general theory of reasons, but also an account of how numbers matter, for if there are non-contractualist reasons there are questions about the relevance of numbers within them.

Central to the discussion to follow is the contrast between complete and partial compliance, or conformity with reason.[4] Conforming to reason is potentially a matter of degree. Apart from the two extremes of full or no compliance there are usually possibilities of partial compliance. If I owe you $100 and I give you $60 I do less than I ought to have done, but more than nothing. It would have been better had I given you $100, but worse had I

---

[3] 'Contractualism' here refers to Scanlon's version of it.

[4] I will use these terms interchangeably. That is, I will not assume that 'complying' with reasons requires knowledge of the reasons, nor being motivated by them. Following a reason, on the other hand, is action for the reason, though the reason need not be thought of as a reason (e.g. the love of another may be a reason for people who do not have the concept of a reason).

given you nothing. Why? Because had I given you $100 I would have completely complied with reason (that reason), whereas I did not. And had I given you nothing I would have been further away from complete compliance than I am. Having reasons means that one should comply with them, that is comply perfectly. It also means that it is better to comply partially than not at all, and the closer one is to complete compliance the better. In saying that one is not adding anything to the idea of a reason for action. It is essential to the concept of reason that complete compliance is what it calls for, and that the closer one gets to it the better.

That much is implied by nothing more than the possibility of incomplete compliance, and of the possibility of different degrees of compliance. If we deny that then, if I owe you $100 and do not have it, and therefore cannot do what I have reason to do, I have no reason to give you the $60 which I do have. Of course, I would admit, I should give you $100, but why – given that I cannot – should I give you the $60? It is not what I have reason to do. But I do have a reason to do so. The reason to give you $100 is also a reason to give you $60, given the circumstances.

The difficulty is not in accepting the point but in applying it. Money is, other things being equal, an easy case. But is giving one shoe to a person to whom we owe a pair better than giving him none? It all depends, it may be better, it may be worse, or at any rate not better. Moreover, what appears like partial compliance may be doing something good of a different kind, which cannot count as partial compliance with the original reason at all. Suppose you promised a friend a ticket from London to his brother's wedding in Australia, and instead you give him a bus ticket to Dover. Dover is closer to Australia and a pleasant town. But getting there will not help him in getting to the wedding at all, and the pleasantness of spending time there has nothing to do with the original promise, and cannot count as partial compliance with it.[5] Such cases far from undermining the general point that partial compliance is better than none reinforce it. They show how what constitutes partial compliance is sensitive to an understanding of the reason, and is partial compliance only if it is required by that reason.

---

[5]   Some people regard any specific promise, e.g. to give you Kant's First Critique, as a promise to give something of that value, something which costs as much as Kant's book. They have similar ways of understanding non-voluntary duties. Believing these to be mistaken I disregard them here.

Sometimes incomplete compliance results from complying fully with one reason while failing to comply with another. A parent of two children who looks after one, but neglects the other is failing to comply completely with reason, but his failure would have been greater had he neglected both (other things being equal, as for current purposes we put aside envy, possible hurt to the self-esteem of the neglected child, etc.) More generally, if one has two independent[6] reasons then complying with only one of them is not complete compliance with reason, for the other is not complied with (if the other were the only reason applying one would not be in complete compliance without complying with it, and how could the fact that one complied with another, independent, reason change that?) Yet, compliance with one is partial compliance, as can be seen by the fact that if the other no longer exists or no longer applies, having complied with the one will constitute complete compliance, whereas had one not complied with it one would not be in complete compliance. The same goes for any number of reasons. This too seems to me to be part of what is built into the notion of a reason for action.

The concept of complete compliance is vague. I use it as meaning that during the relevant period the agent completely conformed with each of the reasons which then applied to him. As I use it, it does not refer to how perfect were the agent's motives or intentions, nor to perfection in the manner of complying with reason (swiftly, etc.) so long as they do not mean that what was done was less than what there was reason to do. I do use it to apply to reasons to refrain from action (not to kill, etc.) These clarifications leave it vague. Some doubts about the concept are reflected in the parental example. I may prefer to have parents who, if they neglect their children at all, neglect all of them, rather than pick and choose. It may speak worse of their character that they pick and choose. However, in discussing complete compliance, this is irrelevant. A parent who neglects only one of his children would be neither a better person, nor a better parent, nor come closer to complete compliance with reason if, having grasped the point just made, he started neglecting his other children as well.

The principles of counting reasons are indeterminate over a vast range of cases. Often, of course, the individuation of reasons

---

[6]   Meaning that compliance with one does not affect the existence, application or stringency of the other.

is important. It matters, e.g. in order to establish whether one reason derives from another, whether they are independent of each other, in order to understand their rationale, and sometimes in order to judge their stringency. However, often the way we individuate reasons is unimportant. What matters is that we comply with reason. It matters little whether we have a single reason or several. Do I have one reason to look after my children, or several, a separate reason to look after each one of them? Who cares? But then complying with each of the reasons for looking after this child or that brings me closer to complying with the one general reason of looking after my children, thus confirming the general principle that *for any reason applying, one is closer to complete compliance with reason if one complies with it than if one does not.*[7]

These observations show that the notion of degrees of compliance does not depend on the possibility of perfect compliance. Perfect compliance may be possible when debt repayment is considered, but if perfect compliance means that nothing can be done which will improve compliance then perhaps there is no perfect compliance with the reasons parents have to care for their children. It may always be possible to do more for one's children. The notion which we require for our discussion is that of *degree of compliance.* That degree depends on three factors. When the reasons applying are independent and of equal importance the more reasons we comply with the closer we come to complete compliance. Our understanding of degree of compliance suggests, however, that it depends on the importance, as well as the number of reasons we comply with, and the degree of compliance with each of them.

These observations also suggest, though it requires further argument to establish the point, that there is one overarching concept at work, namely what we have reason to do, and that separate independent reasons are by their nature contributory factors towards that, constituting what we have reason to do. For example, sometimes it is best, when we are unable to comply perfectly with all the reasons, to comply partially with all of them rather than completely with one and not at all with the others. If I cannot meet all my children's needs it is better to meet all their most essential needs, and leave some less essential needs unmet, rather than meet all the needs of one and none of the needs of

---

[7] It is no exception to this principle that if complying with it makes impossible complying with a more important reason one should comply with the latter.

the others, suggesting the presence of a general notion of conformity with reason to which conformity with each reason contributes. In all, degrees of compliance with reason depend on degrees of compliance with any single applying reason, the number of independently applying reasons one complies with, and their importance. As both the determination of degrees of compliance with single reasons and the ranking of the importance of reasons are very partial, degrees of compliance are often incommensurate.

How could it be otherwise? Assume independent reasons of equal stringency. Assume, to start with, that one has two reasons. Can it be other than that one would conform to reason if one conforms to each of them and will only partly conform if one conforms only to one? To deny that is in effect to claim that conforming with one reason rescinds the other, so that one is in complete conformity with reason having conformed with one only. But that means that the reasons are not independent of each other.

This argument shows that complete conformity requires conforming with all the reasons which apply to one. A similar argument shows that, given our assumption of independence and equal stringency, complying with more brings one closer to complete compliance than complying with fewer. Assume that one has only two reasons. In that case conforming with two is closer to complete compliance than conforming with only one (because it is complete compliance). How can the appearance of another reason change that? Clearly once a third reason appears conforming with the previously existing two is no longer complete compliance with reason. But how can that change the relationship between complying with the one and with the two? How can it change the fact that complying with two is closer to complete compliance than complying with one? We know that for any number of reasons N, if there are no other reasons to comply with on this occasion then (1) complying with N is closer to complete compliance than complying with N minus 1, and (2) complying with N is complete compliance. Suppose that there are further reasons applying to the agent. That would invalidate (2), but how can it invalidate (1)? It does not seem to make sense that it does. These consideration do not show that degrees of compliance also depend on the relative importance of the applying reasons. If need be this dependence can be established via examples.

2. The core argument

That, then, is why the lifeguard would be at fault were he to save only one if he could save many. For the sake of the argument it is assumed that he has, for each drowning person, a reason to save him. Saving all is what he has reason to do. Saving one is only partial compliance with it. If he can comply fully he is at fault if he does not try. The more he saves the closer he is to complete compliance. If he cannot comply fully he should save as many as he can, and he is at fault if he does not try.

Is there no mistake? Surely he has reason to save only those he can save. If he saves the few he cannot save the many. Therefore, he has no reason to save them. This explains the difference between his saving one on the side where there is only one, and saving one only, where there are two near each other which he can save. In that last case if he saves one and stops he is at fault, for he could have saved the other as well. In the two directions case he can save only those in one direction. Once he sets out to save them he cannot save the others, and therefore has no reason to save them. Therefore, he is at fault only if he is at fault to set out in one direction rather than the other. But that, the argument goes, he is not, for either way he will save as many as he can.

This argument fails for two reasons. First, we sometimes have reason to do what we cannot. Finer discrimination is needed to show when inability negates reasons. Second, even if we waive this point the guard would be at fault were he to save the one rather than the many, for he would be at fault not to choose the direction of the many. Regarding any of the drowning people the guard has reason to save them. It is true that he cannot save all. So if there are three drowning people, his reason to save each of three, and at the outset he can save each of them, sums up as a reason to save two, never mind who. He can save two, has a reason to save them, and, as a result will have completely complied with reason (assuming he has no reason to do more than he can) were he to save two. Therefore, he ought to choose the direction of the many, and he is at fault if he does not. His voluntarily and knowingly rendering himself, by choosing the direction of the one, unable to save more than one is no excuse for failing to comply fully with reason.

So much for my core argument that numbers count. It is, of course, an argument that compliance with reason counts, and that means that for any independent reason which applies to agents they come closer to complete compliance if they conform with it than if they do not. As we saw this is sufficient to establish that numbers count in a very restricted class of cases. It does not follow that they do not count in any other way. I do not know of any general argument to establish this negative conclusion. It is not, however, implausible.

Contrast, e.g., reasons to perpetuate the Nation with reasons to save people. Presumably the only way to save the Nation is to save or protect people who do or will belong to it. However, it does not follow that the more people are saved or protected the better. Possibly once a certain number of people are saved, or their life secured, there is no further point in saving or protecting more. That would no longer affect the survival of the nation. It may even be that its survival will be safer with a smaller number of nationals dedicated to its perpetuation, than with a larger number who are more or less indifferent to it, and it may be that, once the threshold of adequacy has been achieved, dedication to the perpetuation of the Nation is in reverse proportion to the number of nationals. On these assumptions the single reason to perpetuate the Nation, if there is such a reason, will not necessarily show the linear sensitivity to numbers that the basic argument establishes regarding the number of equally important and independent reasons, and no alternative route to making numbers count appears on the horizon regarding this case.

Other examples may be more controversial. For example, does the reason we have to respect persons mean that we should strive to extend people's lives as far as possible? I do not believe that it does. Here the more the better does not follow from the argument offered above, nor is it a sensible conclusion to reach. You may disagree with this remark, but the lesson that what matters is what would be a greater degree of respect (the reason relevant in this case) is unaffected by such doubts. It all depends on the nature of the reasons involved. In this example it depends on how far the reasons of respect extend. If so then it is not implausible to think that numbers count only where that brings a higher degree of conformity with reason.

One reaction to the argument above is that it accomplishes nothing. It says, the objection runs, that numbers count if reasons say that they do. We know that. The question whether numbers count is the question whether reasons establish that they count, and the argument above does nothing to answer that question. Up to a point this is of course true. But there is something more to the argument than that. It establishes that to the degree that reasons can be individuated and counted numbers must count, for the number of reasons matters to achieve full conformity to reason.

Just as some may suspect that the argument above does not go far enough so others will fear that it goes too far. Does it not yield the conclusion that we should have two children rather than one? Does it not entail that we should kill one person to use his kidneys to save two? These are natural concerns. But they do not necessarily show that there is anything wrong with the argument I outlined. They may dissolve once we understand correctly the reasons which seem to give rise to them. Alternatively, they may be resolved by the presence of additional factors and principles, ones we have not considered. Scanlon draws on such additional principles.

3. The aims of Contractualism

To examine his way with aggregation, with the ways numbers count, we need to consider briefly the aims of Contractualism. As he sees it Contractualism contributes in several, inter-related ways. It establishes a connection between wrong-making reasons and a special kind of motivation, the motivation to act on principles which similarly motivated people cannot reasonably reject. It explains what unifies a central area of morality, that of wrong-making reasons. It provides a common focus for thought, and a framework for arguments on these matters. But Contractualist arguments do more than explain independently existing reasons. They constitute wrong-making reasons. Contractualist arguments are the reasons why certain actions are owed to others, and other actions are wrong.[8] This makes Contractualism a constructivist theory.

---

[8]   Replying to Thomson, Scanlon writes: 'the contractualist formula . . . is intended as an account of what it is for an act to be wrong. What *makes* an act wrong are the properties that would make any principle that allow [sic] it one that it would be reasonable to reject' (391n21). Naturally, he is not saying that 'wrong' means 'ruled out by a principle which no one can reasonably reject'. But neither is he saying that the formula merely theoretically classifies actions we should not do into wrong ones and, say, merely ill-advised ones. For Scanlon, a wrong-making reason defeats reasons of all other kinds. There are, therefore, specific wrong-making reasons. His way of establishing such reasons is by arguments using the Contractualist formula. Hence the most abstract wrong-making-reason is that the action is prohibited by a principle to which no one can reasonably object, and

This, it is sometimes thought, marks clear water between Contractualist and other accounts of reasons. But the difference is easily exaggerated. Some, myself included, believe that reasons (and values) are inherently intelligible, that it is possible to explain why any specific reason is a reason. When the thesis about the intelligibility of reasons is taken to imply that explanations are always available, it too asserts a constitutive relationship between explanations and reasons, for according to it there are no reasons which cannot be explained. The difference is that constructivists alone hold that there is a master argument which establishes the validity of all moral reasons (or whichever class of reasons one is constructivist about). It alone, or its exemplifications, are reasons of that kind. The thesis about the intelligibility of reasons does not privilege any form of explanation, and is acceptable to those who doubt that one master argument is either available, or necessary to show of any moral reason that it is a reason.

Scanlon may accept the intelligibility of reasons generally. But he thinks that one form of argument has a privileged position in establishing what we owe each other. It is not obvious what is the special privilege. Is it that no other argument can explain what is wrong with rape, or cruelty, or deceit, and so on? That implies either that no one understood what is wrong with such acts until *What We Owe To Each Other*, or at least until Kant, the first constructivist, or that those who did understand were constructivists *manqués*.[9] If there are other explanations for moral reasons then Contractualism does not establish the existence of reasons which cannot be established some other way. Rather, it provides additional arguments for them, arguments which are perhaps the only ones to explain why those reasons are ones we owe each other, and are the only one which provide a full, or 'deep' understanding of why we owe each other what we do. If I am right then Contractualism claims not so much to improve our knowledge of moral wrongs as to deepen our understanding.

This modesty may mislead. While it allows for knowledge of moral right and wrong even by people who reject Contractualism,

---

'this is torture', e.g., instantiates it in particular circumstances. They relate in the way that, e.g., if the only moral principle is to promote the interests of the State, promoting the interests of the State, the most abstract moral reason, relates to not-spying, a concrete reason instatiating it in particular circumstances.

[9]   A third option, that they understood through some intuition which they could not articulate, is ruled out by Scanlon's belief that moral views always come with beliefs in reasons for them: p. 198.

their views are sound only if there are Contractualist arguments which vindicate them. Contractualist arguments are the ultimate arbiter of what we owe each other. This means that Contractualism is successful only if it has the resources to establish moral conclusions, and to do so independently of non-contracualist arguments or reasons. Even before *What We Owe To Each Other* was published critics alleged that it does not. In the book Scanlon squarely faces the objection:

> Deciding whether an action is right or wrong requires a substantive judgment . . . about whether certain objections to possible moral principles would be reasonable. . . . a judgment about the suitability of certain principles to serve as the basis of mutual recognition and accommodation. . . . (T)he idea of what would be reasonable . . . is an idea with moral content. This moral content . . . invites the charge of circularity. By basing itself on reasonableness, it may be charged, a theory builds in moral elements at the start. . . . [E]verything we are to get out of it at the end we must put in at the beginning as part of the moral content of reasonableness. (194)[10]

We see how serious this difficulty is when considering how the Contractualist test works: A principle is proposed, which either permits or prohibits behaving in a certain way, say doing A. It is valid if and only if it passes the Contractualist test which pits it against all possible objections. It does not matter whether these objections are actually advanced by anyone. The principle is valid if and only if no one *can* reasonably object to it, that is only if none of the possible objections are reasonable. Whether the possible objections are reasonable, and justify rejecting the proposed principle, depends on the ways in which people would be burdened by forbidding or permitting an action. Suppose that, compared to the objections to a permissive principle, the objections to the prohibition which its denial entails are not significant. That would establish that it is reasonable to reject the permissive principle, and that the prohibitive principle is valid (195). This test makes the theory Contractualist: any principle is vetoed if there

---

[10] All references are to *What We Owe To Each Other* (Harvard University Press 1998). For an early version of the objection see Pettit, *The Common Mind* (Oxford University Press 1993), 297–302. Pogge's 'What we can reasonably reject' (Sosa & Villanueva (eds.) *Philosophical Issues* 11 (Blackwell 2001), 118–147) shows the difficulties Contractualism encounters should one try to use it to establish concrete moral conclusions, without importing moral premises independently established.

is a reasonable objection someone can raise. The suspicion that the test renders the theory vacuous, or 'circular', arises because what is reasonable is, as Scanlon is aware, a moral matter.

Scanlon is clear that broad areas of morality lie beyond the boundaries of Contractualism.[11] The suspect feature of Contractualism is not that. It is that its test yields results only by presupposing moral views which can only be established independently of it. Is it not the case that those results can be derived from these premises independently of the Contratualist test? Consider Scanlon's discussion of the relevance of the likelihood of burdens and benefits (206–9). He rejects the suggestion that in determining the reasonableness of possible objections to a principle the probability that any particular individual will benefit or be burdened should be ignored (to avoid bias favouring or against that person), but that the percentage of the population likely to benefit or be burdened should be taken into account. He rejects the suggestion because it 'leads to unacceptable results', for 'a contractualist would want to keep open the possibility that [a principle imposing severe hardship on a few for the benefit of many] could be reasonably rejected' (208–9). In brief, you determine the moral outcome in some non-contractualist way, and shape the test to yield the right conclusion, the one you started from, except that now it receives the *imprimatur* of having been established by the Contractualist test.[12]

Whatever we think of his treatment of this example, it does not establish that relying on pre-established moral claims renders Contractualism vacuous. It is vacuous if what you get out of it is what you put in as premises, without Contractualism itself making a difference to our moral conclusions. Michael Ridge argued that Contractualism is not merely an 'unhelpful epicycle' because it makes a difference by barring certain considerations from

[11]   Pp. 171–187. Scanlon's observation that 'contractualism . . . is not meant to characterise everything that can be called 'moral' but only that part of the moral sphere that is marked out by certain specific ideas of right and wrong' is meant to address three different cases: (1) false beliefs about what is moral or immoral, e.g., that masturbation is immoral; (2) cases falling outside Contractualism proper, but which can be covered by certain extensions of it (the 'trusteeship' idea p. 183); (3) cases of moral concerns lying outside the scope of the Contractualist test.
[12]   Does not the reference to 'a contractualist' in the quote suggest that there are Contractualist arguments to that conclusion? None is provided. Scanlon's subtle discussion shows that the principle which yields the outcomes which he, for reasons not given, believes are right, is consistent with Contractualism, not that the alternatives are inconsistent with it. They simply do not deliver the wished-for results.

affecting the outcome of the Contractualist test. Scanlon, he claims, does not allow all moral considerations to bear on what objections are reasonable, only agent-relative objections do.[13]

Ridge's suggestion misinterprets Scanlon's observation that 'impersonal reasons do not, themselves, provide grounds for reasonably rejecting a principle' (220). Scanlon's point is that right and wrong are determined by considerations affecting people (and not mountains, or the American condor). He does not, nor should he mean that right and wrong are determined by agent-relative considerations only. People are affected by the impact on them of agent-neutral considerations, and there is no justification to deny the reasonableness of objections based on such facts. To be sure every person can rely only on the effect a principle would have on him. If some principle will, e.g. reduce my educational opportunities, which is a harm because of the agent-neutral value of education, my objection must relate only to my interest in education, and has the weight due to my interest alone, and not to other people's interest in education. But would this save Contractualism from the charge of vacuousness? As we saw, Contractualism does not deem every setback to a person's interests or concerns as grounding a reasonable objection. Whether they ground reasonable objections depends on a comparison of the burdens a principle imposes compared with the burdens imposed by its rejection (195). Hence there is no reason to think that the limitation of the grounds for reasonable objection to personal reasons would affect the outcome, *unless the Contractualist treatment of aggregation affects the outcome.* The success of Contractualism depends on the success of its treatment of aggregation.

4. Contractualist aggregation – the positive argument

That seems to be Scanlon's own view. His reply to the charge that his theory 'builds in moral elements at the start. . . . [E]verything we are to get out of it [the theory] at the end we must put in at the beginning as part of the moral content of reasonableness' lies in the way all Contractualism privileges the reasons of individuals. Contractualism insists

---

[13] 'Saving Scanlon: Contractualism and Agent-Relativity', *The Journal of Political Philosophy*, 9, (2001), 472.

that the justifiability of a moral principle depends only on various *individuals'* reasons for objecting to that principle and alternatives to it. This feature is central to the guiding idea of contractualism and is also what enables it to provide a clear alternative to utilitarianism and other forms of consequentialism. (229)

Of course, non-contractualists too take account of the concerns of individuals. Does Scanlon privilege each person's reason in a way non-contractualists do not? He does not rely on any claim that a person has special authority regarding how things are normatively from his point of view. His general view suggests that people have no such authority regarding at least some of their own reasons. E.g., they may reasonably object to principles which exempt some people from general duties arbitrarily, and therefore unfairly, even when the exemption does not disadvantage them. In such cases any person, including the people favoured by the principle, can know that the principle is open to that objection, and that it is open to the objection from the point of view of other people as well. No one has special authority in the matter.

Moreover, as this example shows, Scanlon, unlike some Contractualists, does not wish to derive moral reasons from considerations of individuals' well-being. Nor does he give individuals who have sound reasons against a principle a veto over it, as Contractualists generally do. The reasons they have must be considered against reasons for the principle that they and others may also have. Whether anyone has a reasonable objection to a principle depends not only on his or her reasons against it, but on some comparison between their reasons against and the reasons for the principle, given the available alternatives.

In what way, then, does Scanlon privilege individuals' reasons? The answer lies in his treatment of aggregation. Contractualism is not so much an account of moral reasons, as an account of moral aggregation. It is a thesis about the ways in which numbers do and do not determine the outcome of moral conflicts. This is the implication of the fact that Scanlon's treatment of aggregation is his one reply to the charge of vacuity. Scanlon's interest in aggregation was the motive for his initial interest in Contractualism.[14] His success in accounting for aggregation is the key to the success or failure of *What We Owe To Each Other*.

---

[14] See Scanlon, 'Preference and Urgency', *Journal of Philosophy*, 72 (1975) 655; 'Contractualism and Utilitarianism', in Sen & Williams (eds.), *Utilitarianism and Beyond* (Cambridge University Press, 1982), 103.

Scanlon aims to establish that Contractualism would allow for aggregation in some cases and not in others. Here is his argument that 'in cases in which one has a duty of [rescue] . . . and one has to choose between preventing a certain level of injury to either a larger or a smaller number' (232) one must prevent the harm to the larger number. Imagine that the matter is saving life, and the choice is between a group of two and a single person. A principle permitting the rescuer to save the single person ignores the value of saving the life of some people:

{1} Either member of the larger group might complain that this principle did not take account of the value of saving his life, since it permits the agent to decide what to do in the very same way that it would have permitted had he not been present at all, and there was only one person in each group. {2} The fate of the single person is obviously being given positive weight, he might argue, since if that person were not threatened then the agent would have been required to save the two. And the fact that there is one other person who can be saved if and only if the first person is not saved is being given positive weight to balance the value of saving the one. {3} The presence of the additional person, however, makes no difference to what the agent is required to do or to how she is required to go about deciding what to do. {4} This is unacceptable, the person might argue, since his life should be given the same moral significance as anyone else's in this situation (which is, by stipulation, a situation in which no one has a special moral claim). [Endnote omitted]

{5} . . . The conclusion . . . is that any principle dealing with cases of this kind would be reasonably rejected if it did not require agents to treat the claims of each person who could be saved as having the same moral force. Since there is, we are supposing, a positive duty to save in cases in which only one person is present, this means that any nonrejectable principle must direct an agent to recognise a positive reason for saving each person. Since a second reason of this kind can balance the first – turning a situation in which one must save one into one in which it is permissible to save either of two people – the reason presented by the needs of a second person in one of these two groups must at least have the power to break this tie. (232 – numbers between {} added)

Needless to say the conclusion (point {5}) is similar to my conclusions in section 2. Its gist, denuded of its Contractualist
cladding, is that we have separate reasons to save each person.
Where we part company is in the reasons for this conclusion, and
from it to the next step, namely that one must save the two rather
than the one.

Scanlon is clearly right in {4}, special status or relationships
having been excluded by stipulation it follows that the moral significance of each person's life is the same. Scanlon takes this to
imply that the value of each person's life must make a 'difference
to what the agent is required to do or to how she is required to
go about deciding what to do' on every occasion affecting people
({3}, and also {1}). This amounts to denying that a reason is a reason unless it should make a difference to the outcome of deliberation or to the manner of decision (whatever that may mean)
on each occasion to which it applies.

But if so how can Scanlon advance {2}? If I am one of the two,
he says, I can complain that my life is not given any value by the
permissive principle, while maintaining that the life of the single
person is given value. How? His presence turns the agent's duty
to save the two into a permission to save either the single person
or the two. But in objecting to the permissive principle I deny that
the single person's life is entitled to have that effect. I claim that
his presence makes no difference, and there is a duty to save the
two rather than him, as there would be if he were not there. His
situation under the correct principle is exactly like mine under
the permissive principle.[15]

There is no reason to expect a reason to affect either outcome
or manner of decision in every case. If a house is on fire, with
people inside who can be saved only by putting out the fire, it
matters not how many there are. If I save one I save all. One
cannot object that I did not take the life of each person to be of
value, simply because I knew that it makes no difference to the
outcome.

---

[15] Even more so: Scanlon's {1} runs into the following apparent paradox: According to
him both I and the other person in the group of two have a valid complaint that our lives
were not taken to be of value. But if neither of our lives is valuable it follows that only
the single person's life is taken to be valuable and the resulting principle should be a
duty to save him. No such apparent paradox affects the argument that under the correct
principle the single person's life makes no difference to either outcome or mode of
deliberation.

Another problem with the argument turns on the requirement to take each person's life to be of equal value. It is valid, but it does not imply that the value of people's life yields a reason to save them. This is evident once we realise that the permissive principle complies with the requirement. It is consistent with every person's life being such that if it is threatened it should be rescued unless doing so would mean not saving at least one other, in which case respect for each of the endangered lives requires saving at least one. Here every person's life is given a positive and an equal value, but not enough to yield an outright reason to save him or her. Without such reason it is not possible to explain why the correct principle is correct. This, as we saw, is Scanlon's own view.

This point is of some moment, for it rebuts one reason for preferring Scanlon's argument for the principle to mine. I built my argument on the assumption that there is value to human life, and a reason to save lives. I did not argue for these assumptions.[16] Does not Scanlon plug the omission with a Contractualist argument? Unfortunately not. He gives no argument to show that there is a reason to save. That is assumed. His argument is for the equality of the value of people's life. And that equality is established simply by *the assumption* that the people involved have no special moral claims.

I conclude that this argument (231–234) fails to establish that the correct principle is required by Contractualism. In any case there is nothing Contractualist about the argument, except its terminology (one person or another objecting). The whole passage can be recast in noncontractualist terms without losing any of its content or force. This may show that Scanlon's views and mine are closer than may otherwise appear, except that I do not rely on the unhelpful equality argument.

My comments so far do not challenge the Contractualist enterprise. As mentioned already, Contractualism must presuppose ways of dealing with aggregation independent of it. It is natural to assume that they apply to Contractualist reasons as well, unless blocked by Contractualist arguments. Scanlon's argument criticised above aims to show that Contractualism does not go too far in blocking aggregation. To do this Scanlon need not establish Contractualist reasons for aggregation (as he aims to do). It is

---

[16]   I offered some arguments in *Value, Respect and Attachment* (Cambridge University Press 2001) ch. 4.

enough for him to show that Contractualism does not block sensible aggregative moves sanctioned independently of it. I agree
that it does not. The question is, does it block any aggregative
moves? Does it succeed in ruling out aggregation where aggregation should be ruled out?

5. Contractualism against aggregation

Scanlon's guiding principle regarding aggregation is:

> In situations in which aid is required and in which one must
> choose between aiding a larger or a smaller number of people
> all of whom face harms of comparable moral importance, one
> must aid the larger number. (238)

It is this principle which requires the rescue of the two rather than
the one, and it is this principle which, I claimed, is not established
by Scanlon through a Contractualist argument, an argument not
available to non-contractualists. The principle itself is, I believe,
sound, but it does not block any form of aggregation. To block
all other forms of aggregation the most sensible *anti-aggregation
principle* would be:

> In situations in which aid is required and in which one must
> choose between aiding a larger or a smaller number of people
> who face harms which are not of comparable moral impor-
> tance numbers do not matter, and one must aid those facing
> the harm of greater moral importance, even if this means not
> aiding a larger number of people facing harms of a smaller
> moral importance.

I am not sure whether this principle is sound, nor is Scanlon.[17]
But my interest is not in its merits, but only in the question
whether Contractualist arguments can establish it, and can do so
without begging the crucial questions. To explain my doubts I
need not do more than follow Scanlon's own discussion.

The principle relies on a classification of the moral importance
of different harms, and Scanlon implicitly acknowledges that
Contractualism, while presupposing such a classification, con-

---

[17] The nearest he comes to this is in a less explicit and apparently narrower formulation: 'Contractualism does not . . . permit one to save a larger number of people from
minor harms rather than a smaller number who face much more serious injuries.' (238).

tributes nothing to establish it. The very important moral question of what matters and how much, morally speaking, is one to which Contractualism itself has no answer. Contractualism does, however, aim to help with aggregation. One objection to the anti-aggregation principle which Scanlon considers is:

> It may seem that there are harms such that, although it would not be permissible to save one person from this harm rather than to save someone from drowning, nonetheless an agent would be permitted, perhaps even required, to prevent a very large number of people from suffering it, even if that meant that she would be unable to save a drowning person. . . . perhaps blindness and total paralysis are examples of such harms. (239)

Scanlon does not feel able to reject the view that in a choice between saving many from paralysis or one from death it is permitted, or even required to save the many. To accommodate this with Contractualism he feels that he has to reject the anti-aggregation in favour of weaker principles barring impermissible aggregation. He considers a distinction between harms by their relevance to each other:

> If one harm, though not as serious as another, is nonetheless serious enough to be morally 'relevant' to it, then it is appropriate, in deciding whether to prevent more serious harms at the cost of not being able to prevent a greater number of less serious ones, to take into account the number of harms involved on each side. But if one harm is not only less serious than, but not even 'relevant to', some greater one, then we do not need to take the number of people who would suffer these two harms into account. (239–240)

Can this suggestion be justified on Contractualist grounds? Perhaps, he says, the person facing paralysis could reasonably reject a principle requiring saving a single life rather than a large number of people from paralysis on the ground that

> it did not give proper consideration to his admittedly less serious, but still morally relevant, loss. One might then argue that such an individual's claim to have his or her harm taken into account can be met only by a principle that is sensitive to the numbers of people involved on each side. I am not certain how such an argument would go, but it does not seem to me

to be excluded in advance by the general idea of contractualism. (240–241)

And that is the problem. The problem is that Scanlon's Contractualism does not exclude arguments of that form. It means that
a person can object to a principle if, by disallowing aggregation
where it is required, the principle does not give that person's
harm the weight or role that it merits. And that means that the
problem of aggregation has to be solved first, and Contractualist
arguments far from contributing to its solution cannot be
deployed until it is solved.

Scanlon's conclusion (241) is plausible. All he claims is that
the Contractualist position on aggregation maintains that only
the legitimate concern of individuals can count in deciding the
soundness of moral principles. If that is meant to rule out
the thought that 'morality is most fundamentally concerned with
producing the greatest possible benefit' (241) one should agree,
but wonder whether Contractualism helps in establishing the
claim.

It may be that Scanlon's line of thought, based on distinguishing broad categories of moral importance of harms and benefits,
and between harms which are relevant and those which are irrelevant to other harms points in the right (non-contractualist)
direction. It may set relevant questions when considering whether
to help the few or the many.[18] Contractualism, however, offers no
help in answering them.

References

Pettit, Philip (1993). *The Common Mind* (Oxford: Oxford University Press).
Pogge, Thomas (2001). 'What We Can Reasonably Reject', Sosa & Villanueva (eds.), *Philo-
    sophical Issues*, vol. 11, (Oxford: Blackwell) 118–47.
Raz, Joseph (1999). *Engaging Reason: On the Theory of Value and Action* (Oxford: Oxford
    University Press).
—— (2001). *Value, Respect and Attachment* (Cambridge: Cambridge University Press).
Ridge, Michael (2001). 'Saving Scanlon: Contractualism and Agent-Relativity', *The Journal
    of Political Philosophy*, 9, 472–81.
Scanlon, T. M. (1998). *What We Owe To Each Other* (Cambridge, Mass.: Harvard University
    Press).
—— (1998). 'Preference and Urgency', *Journal of Philosophy*, 72, 655–69.
—— (1982). 'Contractualism and Utilitarianism', in Sen & Williams (eds.), *Utilitarianism
    and Beyond* (Cambridge: Cambridge University Press) 103–28.

---

[18] Scanlon is aware, of course, that there are other issues where numbers matter, which
are not directly helped by these ideas.

JUSTIFIABILITY TO EACH PERSON

Derek Parfit

According to

Scanlon's Formula: An act is wrong just when, and because, such acts are disallowed by some principle that no one could reasonably reject.

Though 'reasonable' usually means much the same as 'rational', Scanlon uses this word in a different, moral sense. We are unreasonable, in this sense, if we ignore, or give too little weight to, some other people's well-being or moral claims.[1]

Some critics have suggested that, because Scanlon appeals to this sense of 'reasonable', his formula is empty. On this objection, whenever we believe that some act is wrong, we shall believe that people have moral claims not to be treated in this way. We could therefore argue that such acts are disallowed by some principle which no one could reasonably reject, since anyone who rejected this principle would be giving too little weight to people's moral claims not to be treated in this way. Since everyone could claim that the principles which they accept could not be reasonably rejected, Scanlon's Formula would make no difference to our moral thinking.

That is not so. If we reject the principles that disallow certain acts, we are denying that such acts are wrong. This denial would be unreasonable if it would give too little weight to some other people's moral claims. So Scanlon's Formula implies that

(1) an act is wrong when, and because, the denial that such acts are wrong would give too little weight to some people's moral claims.

---

[1] Scanlon does not assume that, when two people disagree, at least one of these people must be being unreasonable. There can be reasonable mistakes. But, if neither person is being unreasonable in rejecting the other's principle, there may be no relevant principle that could not be reasonably rejected, with the result that Scanlon's Formula would fail. So, when Scanlon claims that no one could reasonably reject some principle, he should be taken to mean that anyone who rejected this principle would be making a moral mistake, by failing to recognize or giving too little weight to other people's moral claims, even if this might be a not unreasonable mistake.

If we accept (1), we cannot also claim that

(2) people have moral claims not to be treated in some way, because such acts are wrong.

People cannot have these moral claims because the denial that such acts are wrong gives too little weight to these claims.

To illustrate this point, suppose that, in

Earthquake. You and Black are trapped in burning wreckage. We are potential rescuers. We could save Black's life, but only by causing you to lose an arm.

On one view about such cases, which we can call

the Greater Burden Principle. We are permitted to impose a burden on someone if that is our only way of saving someone else from a much greater burden.

According to

the Means Principle. It is wrong to inflict great injuries on some people as a means of saving others from greater injuries.

Scanlon makes various claims about what would be reasonable grounds for rejecting moral principles. According to one such claim,

it would be unreasonable . . . to reject a principle because it imposed a burden on you when every alternative principle would impose much greater burdens on others.[2]

Black might say that, as this claim implies, you could not reasonably reject the Greater Burden Principle. Though our following this principle would impose a burden on you, our following the Means Principle would impose a much greater burden on Black. Losing an arm is much less bad than dying.

You might reply that, in your opinion, Black could not reasonably reject the Means Principle. But why would this rejection be unreasonable? You might say that you have a right not to be seriously injured as a means of benefiting someone else. But, in claiming that you have this right, you would be appealing to your belief that it would be wrong for us to injure you in this way. And on Scanlon's view, as we have seen, you cannot appeal to such beliefs. According to Scanlon's Formula,

---

[2]   'Contractualism and Utilitarianism', in *Moral Discourse and Practice*, edited by Stephen Darwall, Allan Gibbard and Peter Railton (OUP, 1997) p. 272.

(3) if it is wrong to inflict such injuries, that is because the Means Principle cannot be reasonably rejected.

If you accept (3), you cannot also claim that

(4) the Means Principle cannot be reasonably rejected because it is wrong to inflict such injuries.

Combining these claims would be like pulling on your boot laces to hold yourself in mid air. If certain acts are wrong because they are condemned by some unrejectable principle, this principle cannot be unrejectable because such acts are wrong.

As this example shows, if we accept Scanlon's contractualism, that makes some moral beliefs easier to defend, and makes others harder to defend. When Black defends the Greater Burden Principle, she can claim that dying is much worse than losing an arm. This is the kind of fact to which, on Scanlon's view, moral reasoning can appeal. When you defend the Means Principle, you cannot appeal to such a fact. Your problem is that, unlike the Greater Burden Principle, the Means Principle is best defended by appealing to our moral intuitions. When we consider cases of this kind, most of us believe that it it is wrong to injure some people, without their consent, as a means of benefiting others. If we think about morality in Scanlon's way, we cannot appeal to such intuitive beliefs. According to what we can call this

moral beliefs restriction, when we apply Scanlon's Formula, we cannot reject moral principles by appealing to our beliefs about which acts are wrong.[3]

This feature of Scanlon's view has wide implications. For example, according to

Act Consequentialism: We ought to do whatever would make things go best.

This view is best challenged by appealing to our moral intuitions. Most of us believe that it can be wrong to act in certain ways – such as killing, lying, or stealing – even when such acts would make things go best. But, if we all accepted Scanlon's Formula, Act Consequentialists could dismiss these appeals to our intuitions.

---

[3]   Thomas Scanlon, *What We Owe To Each Other* (Harvard University Press, 1998), 4–5, 216. Simple page numbers below will refer to this book.

According to

Rule Consequentialism: We ought to act on the principles whose acceptance would make things go best.

If we accepted Scanlon's Formula, Rule Consequentialists could argue:

We ought to act on the principles that no one could reasonably reject. No one could reasonably reject any of the principles whose acceptance would make things go best.

Therefore

These are the principles on which we ought to act.

Scanlon believes that both forms of consequentialism are mistaken. Partly for this reason, he imposes another restriction on grounds for rejecting moral principles. According to what we can call Scanlon's

anti-consequentialist restriction: We cannot reasonably reject some principle by appealing to claims about the goodness of outcomes.

Such claims, Scanlon writes, 'do not provide, in themselves, reason for rejecting principles.'[4] If we cannot reject principles by appealing to such claims, consequentialism is undermined.

According to

Act Utilitarianism: We ought to do whatever would benefit people most.

This view need not make claims about the goodness of outcomes. If Act Utilitarians make no such claims, their view is not undermined by Scanlon's anti-consequentialist restriction. And, if we accepted Scanlon's Formula, these people could dismiss the strongest objections to their view. As Scanlon writes,

the implications of act utilitarianism are wildly at variance with firmly held moral convictions.[5]

On Scanlon's account of moral reasoning, we cannot reject a moral view by appealing to such convictions.

---

[4]   222.
[5]   'Contractualism and Utilitarianism', 267.

According to

Rule Utilitarianism: We ought to act on the principles whose acceptance would benefit people most.

As before, this view need not make claims about the goodness of outcomes. And, if we accepted Scanlon's Formula, Rule Utilitarians could argue:

We ought to act on the principles that no one could reasonably reject. No one could reasonably reject any of the principles whose acceptance would benefit people most.

Therefore

These are the principles on which we ought to act.

Scanlon believes that both forms of utilitarianism are mistaken. Partly for this reason, he adds a further claim about grounds for reasonable rejection. According to what we can call Scanlon's

Individualist Restriction: In rejecting some moral principle, we must appeal to this principle's implications only for ourselves, or for any other *single* person.

In Scanlon's words:

the justifiability of a moral principle depends only on *individuals'* reasons for objecting to that principle and alternatives to it.[6]

This restriction undermines the argument just given. Even if some principle is one of those whose acceptance would benefit people most, there may be people who could reasonably reject this principle. These people may have personal reasons to reject this principle which are stronger than anyone's reasons to reject some alternative.

Scanlon makes several claims about personal reasons for rejecting principles. The strength of these reasons depends in part, as we have seen, on how great the burdens are that some principle's acceptance would impose on us. But it may also depend on certain other facts, such as how badly off we are, or whether we would be responsible for the burdens that would be imposed on us. Some reasons for rejecting principles, Scanlon adds, have

[6]   229.

nothing to do with our well-being. Such reason might be provided, for example, by some principle's unfairness to us.[7] And this list may be incomplete, since reflection may lead us to recognize other reasonable grounds for rejecting moral principles.

Scanlon's view has great appeal. 'What is basic to contractualism', Scanlon writes, 'is the idea of justifiability to each person'. If some act is unjustifiable to other people, that seems enough to make this act wrong. And it seems plausible that, as Scanlon claims, our acts are justifiable to each person only when, and because, we are following principles that no one could reasonably reject.

Should we accept Scanlon's view?

2

One of Scanlon's aims is to provide 'a clear account of the foundations of non-utilitarian moral reasoning'.[8] It is Scanlon's Individualist Restriction, he assumes, that does most to achieve this aim.

Rawls similarly claims that his version of contractualism provides an argument against utilitarianism. This argument, I believe, does not succeed. According to one version of veil of ignorance contractualism, the contractors are told to suppose that they have an equal chance of being in anyone's position. As several writers have claimed, Rawls has no objection to this *equal chance formula* except that it leads to broadly utilitarian conclusions.

It may seem that, in imposing his Individualist Restriction, Scanlon follows Rawls in giving only a question-begging argument against utilitarianism. But this objection can be partly answered. On Rawls's proposed replacement for our ordinary moral thinking, we ensure impartiality by appealing to the principles that it would be rational for us to choose if we didn't know who we were. Nothing in this idea counts against supposing that we have an equal chance of being anyone. As a way of achieving impartiality, this proposal could not be bettered. That is why veil-of-ignorance contractualism provides no argument against utilitarianism.

On Scanlon's version of contractualism, we appeal instead to the principles that no one, given full information, could reason-

[7] 212, and elsewhere.
[8] 'Contractualism and Utilitarianism', 267. He also says that he is one of those 'who look to contractualism specifically as a way of avoiding utilitarianism', 215.

ably reject. This idea does not itself imply that grounds for rejecting principles are provided only by what Scanlon calls 'individuals' reasons'. It does not seem unreasonable to reject some principle by appealing to the burdens that this principle would impose on some group of people. But Scanlon's Individualist Restriction, which excludes such appeals, does not merely beg the question. Since we are asking which are the principles that *no one* could reasonably reject, we must consider each person's reasons for rejecting some principle, and these reasons can plausibly be claimed to be provided by this principle's implications for *this* person. Unlike Rawls's rejection of the equal chance formula, Scanlon's Individualist Restriction is given some support by the rest of his account of moral reasoning.

Scanlon also claims that, by appealing to this restriction, we can reject utilitarianism 'in what seems, intuitively, to be the right way'.[9] Utilitarians reach unacceptable conclusions, Scanlon assumes, because they mistakenly add together different people's benefits and burdens. That is why utilitarians believe that it would be right to impose great burdens on some people whenever that would bring small benefits to a sufficient number of other people.

To avoid such conclusions, Scanlon believes, we should claim that benefits to different people cannot be morally summed. In Scanlon's words:

A contractualist theory, in which all objections to a principle must be raised by individuals, blocks such justifications in an intuitively appealing way. It allows the intuitively compelling complaints of those who are severely burdened to be heard, while, on the other side, the sum of the smaller benefits to others has no justificatory weight, since there is no individual who enjoys these benefits...[10]

There is, I shall argue, another, better response to utilitarianism. This alternative is suggested by Scanlon himself, and is also well supported by the contractualist idea of justifiability to each person. If Scanlon dropped his Individualist Restriction, and developed this alternative, this revision would only add to the plausibility and strength of Scanlon's theory.

[9] 241.
[10] 230.

In arguing for this revision of Scanlon's view, I shall appeal to
what we could plausibly believe about the wrongness of certain
kinds of act. It may be objected that, when we apply Scanlon's
Formula, we cannot appeal to such beliefs. But I shall be discussing, not what is implied by Scanlon's Formula, but Scanlon's
defence of his Individualist Restriction. Scanlon supports this
restriction by appealing to our beliefs about the wrongness of
certain acts in some imagined cases. In one such case,

> *Jones* has suffered an accident in the transmitter room of a tel-
> evision station. To save Jones from an hour of severe pain, we
> would have to cancel part of the broadcast of a football game,
> which is giving pleasure to very many people.[11]

Scanlon claims that, in this case, the numbers would not count.
Even if a billion people were watching this game, we ought to
interrupt their pleasure for the sake of saving Jones from his hour
of pain. Since Scanlon defends his Individualist Restriction by
appealing to our intuitions about particular cases, I shall also
appeal to such intuitions.

In most of the cases that I shall discuss, there are people who
need help, and we must decide whom to help. None of these
people, we should assume, has any special claim to be helped, nor
do these people differ in any other morally relevant way.

According to Scanlon's Individualist Restriction, benefits to different people cannot be morally summed. On what we can call
the *pure anti-numbers view*, it is always irrelevant how many people
our acts could affect. In choosing between any two acts, we should
take into account only the strongest claim that anyone has that
we act in one of these ways, and the strongest claim that anyone
has that we act in the other way. It makes no difference how many
people have these strongest claims, and we can ignore all weaker
claims. Every choice can thus be regarded as if it would affect only
two people.

This view, Scanlon believes, is too extreme. On the view that
Scanlon defends, which we can call

> *the Tie-breaker View.* When the strongest opposing claims are
> roughly equally strong, numbers break ties, and we ought to
> do what would meet the claims of more people.[12]

---

[11]   235.
[12]   240.

To assess this view, consider

> *Life Boat*: White is stranded on one rock, and five people are stranded on another. Before the rising tide covers both rocks, we could use a life boat to save either White or the five.

These six people, we should suppose, would all get the same benefits from the saving of their lives. On Scanlon's Tie-breaker View, since these benefits are equal, the numbers count. We ought to save the five rather than White.

White could challenge this conclusion. We can reasonably reject some principle, Scanlon claims, if we have personal reasons to reject this principle which are stronger than anyone's reasons to reject some alternative. The strength of our reasons to reject some principle depends mainly on how great the burdens are that this principle's acceptance would impose on us. And we count as burdened if we are denied some possible benefit. On these assumptions, White could reasonably reject the Tie-breaker View. According to

> *The Equal Chance Principle*: When we could give equal benefits either to some people or to others, we ought to give everyone an equal chance of getting these benefits.

White's objection to the Tie-breaker View is stronger than anyone's objection to this alternative. If we acted on the Tie-breaker View, that would impose on White the great burden of certain death. If we acted on the Equal Chance Principle, that would not impose on anyone as great a burden.

When Scanlon considers a similar principle, he writes:

> it might be argued that the strongest grounds for rejecting this principle are weaker than the strongest grounds for rejecting the principle of saving the greater number, since whoever loses out under this principle has at least been given a chance of being saved. The argument is not persuasive, however. Whichever of these principles is followed, the ultimate stakes for the people affected are the same: some will suffer severe harm, the others will be saved.[13]

These remarks assume that, when we compare different principles, we should ignore people's chances of avoiding burdens, or

---

[13]   233.

receiving benefits, since the chance of some benefit is not itself a benefit. White cannot claim that, if we give her a chance of being saved, that would be better for her. She might be unlucky; and, if she were, she would have gained nothing.

These remarks do not, I believe, answer White's argument. Though the chance of a benefit is not itself a benefit, we should not ignore such chances. We should take into account people's *expected* benefits, which are the possible benefits that these people might receive, divided by the chances that they would receive them. On the simplest view, which is at least roughly right, expected benefits matter as much as benefits that are certain. Suppose that, in some medical example, our alternatives are these:

| We treat Green | Green will certainly live for one more year | Grey will die now |
| We treat Grey | Green will die now | Grey will have a one in two chance of living for another forty years |

As Scanlon would agree, we ought here to treat Grey. We could give Grey an expected benefit of another twenty years of life, and that expected benefit is much greater than the certain benefit of one extra year that we could give to Green. Green's benefit, we can add, would not in fact be certain. We could at most give Green a high probability of living for one more year, and that is a lesser expected benefit than Grey's one in two chance of living for another forty years.

Return now to White and the five. While the Tie-breaker View would impose on White the burden of certain death, the Equal Chance Principle would impose on everyone only a one in two chance of death. Compared with the certainty of death, that chance would be a significantly smaller expected burden. So, on Scanlon's Individualist Restriction, White can reasonably reject the Tie-breaker View. White's personal reasons for rejecting this view are significantly stronger than anyone's reasons for rejecting the Equal Chance Principle.

We can draw a wider conclusion. On Scanlon's assumptions, we should always follow the Equal Chance Principle. Whenever we could give equal benefits either to some people or to others, we ought to give everyone an equal chance of getting these benefits, since that is always what would make the greatest individual burden as small as possible. In all such cases, it is only the Equal Chance Principle that no one could reasonably reject.

Scanlon is right, however, to reject this principle. It would be wrong to toss a coin, giving White her chance of being saved, since that would also be a chance that we would save four fewer lives. As Scanlon's Tie-breaker View implies, we ought to save the five.

To defend this view, I believe, Scanlon must give up his Individualist Restriction. The five must be allowed to argue that, though White's personal reason to reject the Tie-breaker View is stronger than any of their reasons to reject the Equal Chance Principle, their five reasons *together* outweigh White's.

Return next to Scanlon's claim that, when one person's burden would bring small benefits to others,

> the sum of the smaller benefits to others has no justificatory weight, since there is no individual who enjoys these benefits.

White could similarly claim that, though our saving of the five would give them a sum of benefits that is greater than the single benefit that we could give White, this sum of benefits has no justificatory weight, since there is no one who would enjoy these benefits. If we saved the five, none of them would live five lives.

Scanlon gives some other arguments for the Tie-breaker View. These arguments, he claims, preserve 'the individualistic basis of contractualism', since they could be given 'from the standpoints of the individuals involved'. That is true, I believe, only in the sense in which utilitarianism also has an individualistic basis. For example, Scanlon writes

> It would be reasonable to reject a principle . . . that did not give positive weight to each person's life.[14]

As utilitarians might say, 'Each person counts for one. That is why more count for more'.

After defending the Tie-breaker View, Scanlon suggests that, in some cases, numbers can do more than break ties. On this suggestion, which we can call

> *the Close Enough View.* When burdens to different people are close enough in size, one greater burden could be morally outweighed by a sufficient number of lesser burdens.

[14] 233.

This view might be combined with the assumption that, when burdens are close enough, their moral importance is proportional to their size. That is what utilitarians believe. Utilitarians merely add that *all* burdens are close enough, so that every burden's importance is proportional to its size.

Scanlon seems to make a different assumption. When he describes the Close Enough View, Scanlon writes,

> it could be wrong to save one person's life when we could instead have prevented a million people ... from becoming paralysed.[15]

For most people, becoming completely paralysed would be at least a twentieth as bad as dying. If the importance of these burdens were proportional to their size, one person's death would be morally outweighed by as few as thirty or forty people's becoming paralysed. Since Scanlon chooses the much larger number of a million people, he seems to give these lesser burdens much less weight. On what we can call this

Disproportional View. Lesser burdens should be discounted, since their moral importance is less than proportional to their size.

We now have four views to consider. On Scanlon's Individualist Restriction, different people's burdens cannot be morally summed. On the Tie-breaker View, when we must choose whom to save from equally great burdens, numbers can break ties. On the Close Enough and Disproportional Views, great burdens can be outweighed by many lesser burdens that are close enough in size, but these lesser burdens have disproportionately less weight.

There is, I believe, a decisive objection to all these views. Scanlon defends his Individualist Restriction as the best way to avoid some unacceptable utilitarian conclusions. According to utilitarians, it can be right to let some people bear great burdens for the sake of giving small benefits to enough other people. Scanlon plausibly assumes that, in some such cases, we ought to reject this view. But, as I shall now argue, Scanlon's description of these cases misidentifies their morally relevant features. As a result, he rejects utilitarianism for the wrong reason. Utilitarians

[15]   239–40.

go astray, not by letting the numbers count, but by ignoring or rejecting all principles of distributive justice.

3

In the cases that are most relevant here, there are several people whom we could easily help, and we must choose whom to help. In some cases of this kind, if we don't intervene, some of the people whom we could help would be worse off than others. In such cases, we can say, the *baseline* is *unequal.*

Suppose that, in *Case One,* various people have painful diseases. With our scarce medical resources, we cannot treat all these people. The only possible outcomes are these:

		Future weeks of pain	
		for Blue	for each of some number of other people
	do nothing	100	10
We	do (A)	100	0
	do (B)	0	10

According to utilitarians, if the number of other people was eleven, we ought to choose (A), since that is how we could produce the greatest sum of benefits. Most of us would disagree, believing that we ought to save Blue from her great ordeal. We may even believe that, whatever the number of these other people, we ought to benefit Blue rather than them.

Scanlon suggests three ways of defending such beliefs. According to the Individualist Restriction, Blue could reasonably reject all principles that permitted us to choose (A), since these principles would impose a burden on Blue that is much greater than the burden imposed on anyone by principles requiring us to choose (B). According to one version of the Close Enough View, Blue's benefit of a hundred pain-free weeks could not be morally outweighed by ten pain-free weeks for any number of the other people, since the size of these lesser benefits is not close enough. According to the Disproportional View, even if these lesser benefits are close enough, they should be discounted. We ought to benefit Blue rather than giving these lesser benefits to twenty, or a hundred, or even more other people.

These views are all, I believe, mistaken. If we ought to benefit Blue rather than these other people, that is not because we would be giving Blue a greater benefit. It is because, without this benefit, Blue would suffer more than these other people.

That can be shown by removing this feature of the case. Suppose that, in *Case Two*, our alternatives are these:

		Future weeks of pain for Blue	for each of some number of other people
	do nothing	100	10
We	do (A)	100	0
	do (B)	0	10

In this version of the case, the baseline is equal. If we don't intervene, all these people would be equally badly off, since they would all suffer as much. On Scanlon's Individualist Restriction, since benefits to different people cannot be morally summed, we ought again to choose (B), giving Blue her greater benefit. It makes no difference how many other people we could save from part of their ordeal. We ought to give Blue her hundred pain-free weeks rather than giving ten pain-free weeks to each of as many as a *million* other people. That is very hard to believe.

One objection to this view is that, if we gave Blue her greater benefit, the outcome would be much worse, since there would be much more suffering. To find this objection forceful, we need not be act consequentialists, who believe that we should never choose the worse of two outcomes. It is enough to be *semi-consequentialists*, who believe that some acts are wrong because their outcomes are so bad. Most of us would believe that, in this example, we ought to save a million of these other people from ten of their weeks of pain.

Scanlon is a *pure anti-consequentialist*, since he believes that the wrongness of acts never depends on the badness of their outcomes. Of those who hold such views, most reject the idea that some outcomes are worse than others. That is not Scanlon's view. Scanlon believes that it would be worse if more people suffer or die. But, on Scanlon's account of moral reasoning, the badness of outcomes is morally irrelevant.

Scanlon knew that he was telling us to ignore such badness. But my example has another feature, whose importance Scanlon seems to have overlooked. If we gave Blue her greater benefit, we would not merely be failing to prevent vastly more suffering. This suffering would come to people who would all, without our help, suffer just as much as Blue. In such cases, I believe, Scanlon's view conflicts with all acceptable views about distributive justice.

It will be enough to consider two such views. On both views, though we always have a moral reason to produce the greatest net sum of benefits minus burdens, it also matters how benefits and burdens would be distributed between different people. According to *egalitarians*, we should give some weight to equality of distribution. On the *Priority View*, benefiting people matters more the worse off the people are to whom these benefits would go. On this view, if we gave Blue her hundred pain-free weeks, most of this benefit would matter less than the benefits that we could give to each of the other people. Compared with reducing each of these people's burdens from a hundred weeks of pain to ninety, it would be less important to reduce Blue's burden from ninety weeks to eighty, less important to make a further reduction to seventy, and so on.

If Scanlon dropped his Individualist Restriction, he might appeal to the Close Enough View. And he might claim that, compared with a hundred pain-free weeks, ten such weeks are close enough. That would allow him to claim that, rather than giving this greater benefit to Blue, we ought to give the lesser benefits to a million of the other people. And, if Scanlon appealed to a weak version of the Disproportional View, he might claim that these lesser benefits should not be heavily discounted. That would allow him to claim that, rather than giving the greater benefit to Blue, we ought to give these lesser benefits to as few as a hundred, or fifty, or even twenty of these other people.

These revisions would not, I believe, go far enough. If the importance of these benefits is not proportional to their size, it is not these lesser benefits but Blue's *greater* benefit that should be discounted. As prioritarians claim, we should discount benefits, not when they are smaller, but when they come to people who are relevantly better off. If we gave Blue her greater benefit, she would be far better off than the other people, since they would have a hundred weeks of pain, and she would have none. Rather than giving Blue her hundred pain-free weeks, we ought to give ten such weeks to only ten, or nine, or even fewer of these other people.

It may help to vary the example. Suppose that, in *Case Three*, we could use our limited medical resources to treat either a single person, *Black*, or some number of other people. The possible outcomes are these:

		Black will live to the age of	A million other people will live to
	do nothing	30	30
We	do (A)	30	35
	do (B)	80	30

If benefits to different people cannot be summed, we ought to choose outcome (B), giving Black her fifty more years of life rather than giving five more years to each of the million other people. That is clearly false. And what makes it false is not merely that, compared with fifty years, five million years of life would be a much greater sum of benefits. In outcome (A), these benefits would also be much better distributed between different people. As before, if any of these benefits should be discounted, it is Black's greater benefit. Most of this benefit would come to someone who would already have lived longer than all these other people. Rather than giving Black her fifty more years, we ought to give five more years to only ten, or nine, or even fewer of these other people.[16]

Because utilitarians believe that the importance of all benefits is proportional to their size, they deny that it would be in itself better if benefits were more equally distributed, or if benefits came to people who were worse off. Though this view may be mistaken, utilitarians are at least neutral between different patterns of distribution. In some cases, as we have seen, various versions

---

[16] There is something to be said for choosing (B), since that would allow at least one person to live a complete life. This we might call the qualitative argument for inequality. Though I believe that this argument has force, it does not support the Disproportional View. Consider, for example, *Musical Chairs*: A hundred people will later be at a hundred levels of well-being. There are two possibilities:

(A) Person One is at level 1, Person Two at level 2, and so on.
(B) Person One is at level 100, and everyone else is one level lower down.

On the Disproportional View, we ought to choose (B). If greater gains and losses have an importance that is more than proportional to their size, the single gain to Person One of being ninety nine levels higher must outweigh the ninety nine losses to the others of being one level lower. Suppose next that, in a variant of this case, the alternative to (A) is

(C) Person One is at level 100, Persons Three to a Hundred are one level lower down, but Person Two is *two* levels lower down.

On the Disproportional View, we ought here to choose outcome (C). As before Person One's gain of ninety nine levels, if given disproportionally greater weight, would morally outweigh the combined losses of the other ninety nine people.

In both these cases, I believe, the Disproportional View is mistaken. And there is no qualitative argument for giving Person One her great benefit.

of Scanlon's view favour the less equal distribution. These views have a built-in bias against equality, and against giving priority to those who are worse off. That is not what Scanlon intends. And, as Scanlon would agree, we ought to reject these views.

4

There may seem to be something right in the Close Enough View. According to utilitarians, as Scanlon writes, one person's great burden could be morally outweighed by sufficient benefits to others, 'no matter how small these benefits may be'.[17] Some great burdens, we may believe, could not be morally outweighed by any number of such tiny benefits. These benefits may seem to be what Kamm calls 'irrelevant utilities'.

Before considering this idea, we should note a technical objection to the Close Enough View. Suppose that, for two benefits to be close enough, the lesser benefit must be at least a tenth as great. The Close Enough View would then imply that,

> rather than giving fifty extra years of life to Black, we ought to give five extra years to some number of other people.

Similarly,

> rather than giving five years to these people, we ought to give a single extra year to some larger number of other people.

But this view would also imply that,

> rather than giving these single years to these people, we ought to give fifty extra years to Black.

On this view, we could not avoid acting wrongly. Whatever we do, we ought to have done something else instead. In cases of this kind, that is an unacceptable conclusion.

This view goes astray because *close enough* is not a *transitive* relation. Though one year is close enough to five, and five years are close enough to fifty, one year is not close enough to fifty. If we believe that a great benefit to one person cannot be morally outweighed by any number of much smaller benefits to other people, we cannot appeal to the relative difference in the size of these

---

[17]   230.

benefits. As we have just seen, that could imply that, whatever we do, we ought to have acted differently. But we might appeal to one or more broadly defined absolute thresholds. Nothing above such thresholds, we might claim, could be outweighed by anything below.

Such claims are most plausibly applied to benefits and burdens that are either trivial or imperceptible. For example, we might claim that

(1) we ought to give one person one more year of life rather than lengthening any number of other people's lives by only one minute.

And we might claim that

(2) we ought to save one person from a whole year of pain rather than saving any number of others from one minute of the same pain.

These lesser benefits, we might say, fall below the *triviality threshold*.

These claims, though plausible, are false. A year contains about half a million minutes. Suppose that we are a community of just over a million people, each of whom we could benefit once in the way described by (1). Each of these acts would give one person half a million more minutes of life rather than giving one more minute to each of the million others. Since these effects would be equally distributed, these acts would be worse for everyone. If we always acted in this way, everyone would lose one year of life. Suppose next that we could benefit each person once in the way described by (2). Each of these acts would save one person from half a million minutes of pain rather than saving a million other people from one such minute. As before, these acts would be worse for everyone. If we always acted in this way, everyone would have one more year of pain.

There are several ways in which claims like (1) and (2) may seem plausible. Most of us are bad at judging the significance of large numbers. We may assume that, if one person's extra minute of pain is morally of trivial significance, that is true of a million people's extra minutes. We may also assume that, if some people would bear much greater burdens than others, or lose much more of their well-being, these are the people who would be worst off. That may not be true; and, when it isn't, that changes the relative importance of these burdens. If I gave a million dollars to some aid agency which would divide this sum equally between a hundred million of the world's poorest people, the loss in my well-being might be much greater than the average benefit that a single extra cent would give to each of these other people.[18] But these hundred million benefits would together be much greater than my loss. Since this sum of benefits would both be much greater, and come to people who are much worse off than me, it is morally irrelevant that these benefits would be very small. My dollars would be well spent.

A third mistake is to consider only single acts. Some acts give ourselves significant benefits in ways that impose tiny burdens on very many other people. That is true, for example, of many of the acts that add to the pollution of many people's air, food, and water. When we consider any one such act, the tiny effects on the many other people may seem trivial. It may seem not to matter if such an act imposes costs on others of less than one cent, or reduces the life-expectancy of others by less than one minute. But, when many people act in such ways, these small effects add up. And, when such effects are roughly equally distributed, these acts are worse for almost all of the affected people. In the world as it is now, such acts together impose great burdens on very many people.

Scanlon warns us not to make this third mistake. He discusses a principle that would require us to save one person from an hour of pain at the cost of inconvenience to any number of other people. According to what we can call this

> *Triviality Principle*. We ought to save one person from a great burden rather than saving any number of others from very tiny burdens.

Scanlon claims that, in deciding whether to accept this principle, we should ask whether

> if [it] were generally followed, the consequences for some individuals (intrapersonally aggregated) would be so great as to make it reasonable to reject the principle.

Scanlon is referring here to the way in which, if the following of this principle would repeatedly impose small costs on certain

---

[18] I say 'the average benefit' because there may be some of these people to whom one extra cent would bring no benefit. There may be nothing they could buy with that cent. But there may be other people to whom one extra cent would make a significant differences, as when this would just enable these people to buy some tool, or make some journey, that would give them several later benefits.

people, these costs would together amount to great burdens. If these burdens were great enough, as Scanlon rightly assumes, these people could reasonably reject the Triviality Principle.

Scanlon's view about this principle differs, however, in one way from mine. I believe that, when we assess moral principles, it is often relevant to consider what these principles would imply in cases that are merely possible. In my two imaginary examples, if we always followed the Triviality Principle, that would shorten everyone's life, and give everyone more pain. That is enough, I believe, to refute this principle. Scanlon seems to assume that, in assessing this principle, we should consider only actual cases. After asking the question quoted above, Scanlon writes:

> I do not believe that this is so. It seems to me that we currently follow something close to this principle and that the occasions to which it applies seem sufficiently rare that the costs on each of us are not very significant.

No one could reasonably reject this principle, Scanlon assumes, because there are few actual cases in which anyone can act upon it.

Factual claims of this kind might be enough to defend our adoption of some policy. But they could not defend a moral principle. If we ought to prevent one person's great burden rather than any number of tiny burdens to others, that is always true. When some principle requires us to act in some way, this principle's acceptability cannot depend on whether such acts are often possible. We cannot defend some principle by claiming that, in the world as it is, there is no danger that too many people will act in the way that this principle requires.

We might, however, revise such a principle, so that it requires us to act in this way only if we know that the number of others acting in this way is not too large. Moral principles ought to take this form when it would be best if there were neither too few nor too many people acting in some way. For example, we might be required to join some rescue mission if we knew that more rescuers were needed, but required not to join if we knew that there was no such need, and that our joining would merely obstruct this mission.

On the Triviality Principle, we ought to save one person from a great burden whatever the number of tiny burdens that our act would impose on others. As we have seen, if people often acted in this way, that might be worse for everyone affected, including those whom these acts would save from great burdens. This principle might be revised, so that it required us to act in this way only if we knew that the number of people acting in this way was below some threshold. Even in this form, I am inclined to believe, this principle is indefensible. But, since this revised principle has little importance, and the arguments against it raise difficult questions, I shall not give these arguments here.

5

Discussing his Individualist Restriction, Scanlon writes

> This feature is central to the guiding idea of contractualism, and is also what enables it to provide a clear alternative to utilitarianism . . .[19]

Neither, I believe, is true.

Scanlon's guiding idea is that of justifiability to each person. This idea gives some support to Scanlon's Individualist Restriction. Our acts would be justifiable to each person, Scanlon plausibly assumes, if such acts are permitted by some principle that no one could reasonably reject. When we ask on what grounds anyone might reasonably reject some principle, it seems a plausible suggestion that each person's grounds for rejection are provided by the burdens that this principle would impose on *this* person, and by other such personal reasons. But this suggestion about grounds for rejection is not implied by the idea of justifiability to each person. It would be no less plausible to claim that, in rejecting some principle, each person could appeal to the burdens that this principle would impose not only on her, but also on other people. Scanlon could give up his Individualist Restriction without giving up, or in any way weakening, his idea of justifiability to each person.

Return to *Life Boat*, for example, in which we could save either White or five other people. Scanlon rightly claims that, in such cases, we ought to save the larger number. That claim could be justified to White. We could reasonably expect White to agree that, since everyone's life matters equally, our reasons to save the five morally outweigh our reason to save White. As Scanlon himself writes,

---

[19] 229.

any nonrejectable principle must direct an agent to recognize a positive reason for saving each person ... It would be reasonable to reject a principle ... that did not give positive weight to each person's life ...[20]

Similar claims apply to cases that involve unequal benefits or burdens. Return to the case in which we could either give Black fifty more years of life, or give five more years to each of many other people – people who would all, without our help, die just as young as Black. We could reasonably expect Black to agree that the single benefit to her could be morally outweighed by some number of these lesser benefits to these other people.

Scanlon also believes that, by appealing to his Individualist Restriction, we can avoid some implausible utilitarian conclusions. This belief, I have argued, misdiagnoses how utilitarians reach these conclusions. Utilitarians go astray, not by adding together different people's benefits and burdens, but by rejecting all distributive principles. Given Scanlon's Individualist Restriction, as we have seen, his formula can lead to some conclusions that are at least as implausible, in part because they conflict with all plausible distributive principles.

Scanlon claims that, if he gave up his Individualist Restriction, his contractualist theory would cease to provide 'a clear alternative to utilitarianism'. That, I believe, is not so. Scanlon underestimates what his theory can achieve. If Scanlon dropped his Individualist Restriction, his formula could support various non-utilitarian principles. That would strengthen his theory, and make it provide a better alternative to utilitarianism.[21]

References

Parfit Derek (in preparation). *Wrongness, Rationality, and Reasons* (Oxford: Oxford University Press).

[20] 233.
[21] Scanlon, I believe, should also give up his claim that his contractualism gives an account of wrongness itself. He should claim that, if acts are wrong in his contractualist sense, that makes these acts wrong in various non-contractualist senses. If he gave up his anti-consequentialist restriction, Scanlon could claim that his formula describes the single highest-level property that makes acts wrong in these other senses. Though this version of Scanlon's theory would not be constructivist, that would also make it stronger. Scanlon would allow that, in deciding whether to accept his theory, we could appeal to our beliefs about the wrongness of acts. When we apply Scanlon's Formula, we should bracket these beliefs. But we would here appeal to our beliefs about another question: that of what would

Scanlon T. M. (1997). 'Contractualism and Utilitarianism', in *Moral Discourse and Practice*, edited by Stephen Darwall, Allan Gibbard and Peter Railton (Oxford: Oxford University Press).

—— (1998). *What We Owe To Each Other* (Cambridge, Mass.: Harvard University Press).

be reasonable grounds for rejecting principles. As much of Scanlon's book shows, that would improve our moral reasoning. Scanlon also shows, I believe, that the most important questions are not about wrongness, but about reasons. I shall defend these claims in a book provisionally called *Wrongness, Rationality, and Reasons* (Oxford University Press, in preparation).

6

THE LIMITS OF MORAL CONSTRUCTIVISM

Mark Timmons

Moral contractualism is a type of view in ethics that attempts to justify morality, or at least a part of it, by appealing to some sort of rational or reasonable agreement among individuals.[1] In *What We Owe to Each Other*, T. M. Scanlon defends a contractualist account of that part of morality that concerns our obligations to others, according to which an action is right if and only if it is justifiable to others. Actions that are justifiable to others are ones based on principles upon which all reasonable individuals who are appropriately motivated can agree. Much of Scanlon's book is devoted to spelling out and illustrating the relevant notion of justifiability to others which represents a distinctive account of moral motivation and moral reasoning. But Scanlon also intends his contractualist view to represent an account of the nature of the properties of moral rightness and wrongness. He identifies the property of wrongness with the property of not being justifiable to others. As I shall explain, Scanlon's metaphysical account of moral properties apparently represents a version of moral constructivism: the existence and nature of moral properties (and moral facts in which they figure) are constituted by the agreements that would be reached by appropriately motivated individuals under specified circumstances. Thus, on the reading I shall propose, Scanlon advocates a version of what I will call constructivist contractualism in ethics.

One important goal of Scanlon's contractualism is to accommodate the idea that moral judgments are (or can be) objective in a way that is incompatible with moral relativism. However, as I will argue, there is tension within Scanlon's view. In particular, his

---

[1] 'Contractualism' is Scanlon's term for what is perhaps more often referred to as contractarianism. Henceforth, I will use Scanlon's term for this family of views. My characterization of moral contractualism has to do with the normative enterprise of justifying morality. Some thinkers appeal to contractualist ideas in an attempt to *explain* rather than justify moral norms and principles. For an overview of the contractualist tradition in moral and political philosophy, where the distinction between evaluative and explanatory versions of contractualism is discussed, see Morris 1996 and Sayre-McCord 2000.

contractualist account of moral reasoning, together with his (apparent) commitment to moral constructivism, make his view vulnerable to one or another species of moral relativism that he wishes to avoid. My central aims in this paper are to explain why this is so and what should be done about it. I think there is good reason to avoid relativism, and I find certain elements of Scanlon's contractualism appealing. The culprit, I think, is moral constructivism. Moreover, I think there is reason to be pessimistic about *any* metaphysically substantive account of moral properties and facts. I suggest that some of the attractive elements of Scanlon's view can be preserved and in a way that avoids relativism by situating the view within what I call metaethical minimalism.[2]

Here, then, is my work plan. In section 1, I distinguish moral contractualism from moral constructivism, and then I go on in section 2 to explain why I think Scanlon's view is plausibly interpreted as a version of constructivist contractualism, focusing in particular on what Scanlon has to say about wrongness as a property. In section 3, I raise an old but, I think, forceful dilemma for any such view: either the view leads to massive moral indeterminacy or it is committed to some form of objectionable relativism. In the middle sections 4–8, I explore how well Scanlon's view does in avoiding the horns of this dilemma. I argue that there is reason for pessimism here; that in the end, his view apparently cannot avoid some form of relativism. I then go on in section 9 to briefly consider certain non-constructivist interpretations of Scanlon's contractualism and conclude that none of them offer much metaethical hope. In section 10, I explain how some of the attractive elements of Scanlon's view can be situated within a minimalist metaethical orientation. I wrap things up in section 11.

1. Contractualism and constructivism in ethics

Contractualism and constructivism in ethics are often found in combination, but these views are distinct and should not be confused with one another. As I mentioned at the outset of this paper, moral contractualism is a family of views that attempts to justify

---

[2]   Specifically, those normative moral elements of Scanlon's view that are central to what I will call his 'substantive contractualism' can be preserved within a minimalist metaethical framework.

morality by appealing to some kind of rational or reasonable agreement among those individuals subject to morality's demands. There are many specific versions of the generic view, differing mainly in their philosophical aims and in the account they give of the nature of rational or reasonable agreement. For present purposes, we need not consider contractualism in all of its main varieties, but a few remarks about its guiding aims are necessary in order to distinguish this type of view from moral constructivism.[3]

Issues concerning the 'justification of morality' belong to moral epistemology. And here it is important to distinguish two distinct projects within moral epistemology that a contractualist view might address – projects often not clearly distinguished. One project has as its aim a specification of the content of a correct set of moral principles and the demands they express. This aim represents contractualism as a discovery procedure for arriving at justified moral principles and addresses the question: 'What moral principles (if any) are or can be shown to be correct or likely correct?' Call this the 'content question'. Contractualism may also address the question: 'What normative reason is there to comply with moral demands?' Call this the 'normativity question'. The two aims are distinct, and a contractualist account of the justification of morality might focus exclusively on the content question or on the normativity question.[4] (As I'll explain in the next section, Scanlon's version of contractualism aims to answer both questions.)

Notice that a contractualist account of the justification of moral principles (in reply to the content question) and a contractualist account of the reasons there are to accept and comply with moral principles (in reply to the normativity question) represent fairly abstract formal accounts of the justification of morality. Although contractualism in ethics is associated with non-consequentialist moral theories, a consequentialist might propose a contractualist justification of her consequentialist moral principles and a contractualist account of what reasons there are to comply with moral principles. The contractualist ideal of agreement does not favor

---

[3]   Again, see Morris 1996 and Sayre-McCord 2000 for good discussions of the many varieties of contractualism.

[4]   Sayre-McCord 2000: 254–5, for instance, associates the project of Kantian constructivism with the aim of satisfying the content question and Hobbsian constructivism with the chief aim of satisfying the normativity question.

one normative moral theory over another. Let us call this kind of contractualism 'formal contractualism'. However, Scanlon and others often take constractualism to be opposed to certain normative moral theories, especially versions of consequentialism. So what we may call 'substantive contractualism' represents one way of developing formal contractualism according to which a moral principle is justified only if *each individual* (who is part of the relevant justifying agreement) either does or would agree to the principle in question. This kind of 'distributive justification' is opposed to the kind of aggregative or collective justification characteristic of versions of consequentialism.[5] In section 4, we will examine Scanlon's substantive contractualism in a bit more detail. Let us turn now to moral constructivism.

In keeping with recent metaethical taxonomy, moral constructivism refers to an ontological and related semantic view about the existence and nature of moral properties, facts and truths.[6] Expressed as an ontological position, moral constructivism is the view that there are substantive moral properties and moral facts, but such properties and facts are constituted by (actual or ideal) human attitudes, conventions and the like – call them 'stances'. The associated constructivist semantic thesis maintains that there are moral judgments and principles that are true, but their being true is to be explained by appeal to (actual or ideal) human stances – attitudes, conventions and the like. Talk of 'stance dependence' and 'stance independence' in this context is sometimes understood in different ways by different philosophers. But instead of digressing here, I refer the reader to what others have said on the matter and leave things at a more or less intuitive level.[7] Perhaps some illumination is gained by saying that for the moral constructivist, moral facts, properties and truths are *constituted by* whatever facts about human stances are featured in the account, whereas for a realist such stances are at most *evidence for* independently existing moral properties, facts and truths.

---

[5]   Scanlon takes the idea of distributive justification to be the guiding idea behind his version of contractualism. Scanlon (229) also mentions Parfit's 'complaint model' as a kind of (substantive) contractualism. Unless specified otherwise, all page references are to Scanlon's *What We Owe to Each Other*.

[6]   For a somewhat different contrast between contractualism and constructivism, see Onora O'Neill's contribution to this volume.

[7]   I am using Milo's (1995: 190–3) felicitous terminology of stance dependence/ independence. See also, Brink (1989: 14–23) and Timmons (1999: 34–8).

Contractualism and constructivism are often combined in a metaethical theory. One of the main motivations behind many forms of contractualism involves wanting to avoid commitment to moral realism. Some contractualists propose to justify a substantive morality while remaining as metaethically noncommittal as possible about issues in moral metaphysics and associated semantics. This is metaethical quietism.[8] However, other contractualists, skeptical of moral realism but wanting to give some metaethical story about moral properties, facts, and truths, are attracted to the constructivist idea that moral properties and associated facts are stance-dependent – constructions based on some actual or hypothetical agreement.[9]

Again, those who embrace moral constructivism often develop the view in terms of some sort of hypothetical (rather than actual) agreement among some select set of individuals. Doing so has various advantages, not the least of which is the promise of a reasonable form of moral objectivism: assuming that there is a body of substantive moral principles upon which all hypothetical agents would agree under the specified conditions, the constructivist can maintain that such principles represent a body of objective moral facts and truths.

So, given one of the main motivations behind contractualism and given what appears to many as the most plausible version of constructivism, we find that contractualists tend to be constructivists and vice versa.

But it is important to see that these views are quite distinct and should not be confused. Clearly (from what was said above), one can accept a contractualist moral epistemology and combine it

---

[8]   Rawls apparently advocates this kind of quietism when he writes: 'We try, then, to leave aside philosophical controversies whenever possible, and look for ways to avoid philosophy's longstanding problems. Thus, in what I have called "Kantian constructivism," we try to avoid the problem of truth and the controversy between realism and subjectivism about the status of moral and political values. This form of constructivism neither asserts nor denies these doctrines'. (1985/1999: 395).

[9]   Rawls (1980/1999: 354) expresses the central constructivist ontological claim when he writes, 'The parties in the original position do not agree on what the moral facts are, as if there already were such facts. It is not that, being situated impartially, they have a clear and undistorted view of a prior and independent moral order. Rather (for constructivism), there is no such order, and therefore no such facts apart from the procedure of construction as a whole; the facts are identified by the principles that result [from the procedure]'. So at different times, Rawls has advocated non-quietist and quietist metaethical positions in relation to his version of contractualism. For some discussion of this matter, see Brink 1989: 303–21. See also Milo (1995) for a defense of contractualism that is non-quietist about metaethical issues.

with a version of moral realism. Moreover, an expressivist, who allows that moral judgments and principles can be justified in some nonepistemic sense of the term, can embrace a contractualist view of moral reasoning. In general, then, contractualist moral epistemology itself makes no commitment to one or another view about moral metaphysics and moral semantics.[10]

Perhaps less obviously, one can embrace moral constructivism and reject contractualism. Consider, for instance, a crude version of metaethical subjectivism according to which a moral judgment (made by some particular individual on some occasion) is true just in case (and because) it conforms to the fundamental attitudes of the person making the judgment at the time in question. Facts about the judger's attitudes, then, are what make that person's moral judgments true and constitute the relevant truth-making moral facts. This kind of view is not a version of, or otherwise committed to, contractualism because it does not appeal to any sort of interpersonal agreement and also because it is a position in moral semantics and metaphysics (as I've described it) not moral epistemology.

Moral contractualism, then, is a position within moral epistemology; moral constructivism is a position in moral metaphysics and semantics. Contractualism necessarily features some form of interpersonal agreement at its core; constructivism does not.

Let us now turn to some of the details of Scanlon's view.

2. Scanlon's constructivist contractualism

As I've already noted, Scanlon's contractualism is aimed at answering both the content and normativity questions about morality.[11] Indeed, a central theme in Scanlon's book is the idea that both questions can be given a unified answer – unified in the sense that a properly developed response to one of the questions represents a proper response to the other.

[10] Here I am understanding the subject matter of moral epistemology to address issues about the epistemic justification of moral beliefs and principles – justification in relation to the epistemic goal of truth – and what is often called the 'practical' or 'instrumental' justification of moral beliefs and principles which has to do with goals other than truth. For more on this, see Sinnott-Armstrong 1996.

[11] Scanlon (148) prefers not to cast these questions as ones requiring that we give a 'justification' of morality, since he thinks talk of such justification often presupposes such tasks as giving amoralists reasons for complying with moral requirements that would (given the amoralist's commitments) convince even the amoralist of morality's importance.

What is distinctive about my version of contractualism is that it takes the idea of justifiability to be basic in two ways: this idea provides both a normative basis of the morality of right and wrong and the most general characterization of its content. According to contractualism, when we address our minds to a question of right and wrong, what we are trying to decide is, first and foremost, whether certain principles are ones that no one, if suitably motivated, could reasonably reject (189).

The idea, then, is to explain the rightness or wrongness of an action in terms of the notion of justifiability and do so in a way that yields an account of both morality's content and rational force. (See section 4 below for more detail about Scanlon's notion of justifiability.)

But how are we to interpret judgments about the wrongness of actions? Here is where Scanlon's (apparent) moral constructivism comes into the picture.

In a number of places in his book, Scanlon indicates that certain metaethical issues (particularly regarding matters of moral ontology) can be avoided in developing his contractualist account of moral judgments. This is particularly evident in his discussion of certain metaphysical and related semantical doubts about the existence and nature of normative reasons. Scanlon contrasts what he calls the 'belief' (roughly descriptivist) account of reasons judgments with an expressivist view, but proposes to remain officially neutral in regard to such views, since he doesn't think that anything significant in his contractualist account of morality turns on such semantic issues.[12] In other places, he clearly rejects any form of moral realism and insists that ontological issues in metaethics simply don't arise on his view.

If we could characterize the method of reasoning through which we arrive at judgments of right and wrong, and could explain why there is good reason to give judgments arrived at in this way the kind of importance that moral judgments are normally thought to have, then we would, I believe, have given sufficient answer to the question of the subject matter of right and wrong as well. No interesting question would remain about the ontology of morals – for example about the metaphysical status of moral facts (2).[13]

---

[12] See ch. 2, § 11, esp. 59.
[13] See also, 59, 63–4, and 355.

One might read this passage as advocating a quietist stance about ontological and associated semantic issues in metaethics, but in light of other passages, it is reasonably clear that Scanlon's remark that 'no interesting question would remain' once we develop an adequate account of moral reasoning should be read as saying that no *further* such questions remain given that contractualists can help themselves to a constructivist account of moral ontology. Here is perhaps the clearest passage in which Scanlon commits himself to the view that moral wrongness (and, by implication, moral rightness) is a genuine substantive property of actions.

> Unlike gold and tiger, moral wrongness is not a natural kind; but it is what might be called a normative kind. That is to say, the property of moral wrongness can be identified with a certain normatively significant property which is shared by actions that are wrong and which accounts for their observed normative features, such as the fact that we have reason to avoid such actions, to criticize those who perform them, and so on. (12)

The most generic characterization Scanlon offers of the normative property in question is in terms of an action's not being justifiable to others. He prefers to express his view in terms of the category of wrongness:

S1 An action A is wrong if and only if it is not justifiable to others.

Expressed in terms of a principle of moral rightness (permissibility), we have:

S1* An action A is right if and only if it is justifiable to others.

Scanlon's central project in his book is to spell out the relevant notion of justifiability to others, which he does in terms of the notion of reasonability.

> [J]udgments of right and wrong . . . are judgments about what would be permitted by principles that could not be reasonably rejected, by people who were moved to find principles for the general regulation of behavior that others, similarly motivated, could not reasonably reject. In particular, an act is wrong if and only if any principle that permitted it would be one that could reasonably be rejected by people with the motivation just

described (or, equivalently, if and only if it would be disallowed by any principle that such people could not reasonably reject (4).

The biconditional expressed in the last sentence of this passage, then, represents a property identity claim and is thus supposed to express the essence of the property wrongness.[14]

S2 An act is wrong if and only if any principle that permitted the action could be reasonably rejected by anyone motivated to find principles of mutual governance.[15]

Again, expressed as a principle of moral rightness (permissibility), we have:

S2* An action is right if and only if there is some principle permitting the action that could not be reasonably rejected by anyone motivated to find principles of mutual governance.

Because the very essence of the properties of rightness and wrongness, and thus facts about these properties, are constituted by the attitudes of individuals and, in particular, are constituted by agreements reached by a group of hypothetical agents under certain specified conditions, Scanlon's contractualism is a version of moral constructivism.[16]

So the idea is this. On a constructivist reading of Scanlon, the truth or correctness of a moral principle is to be explained in terms of a hypothetical agreement among the relevant set of

[14] Although competing moral theories such as utilitarianism, divine command theory, versions of contractualism and other, rival theories are often interpreted as featuring basic moral principles that specify those right and wrong-making features of actions, Scanlon argues that 'contractualism and these other views are better described as rival accounts of the property of moral wrongness itself, rather than as differing accounts of the conditions under which actions have that property' (11–12).
[15] In his book, Scanlon sometimes uses the term 'hypothetical agreement' in characterizing his view, and so his view can alternatively be expressed as claiming that the rightness or wrongness of an action depends on whether principles permitting the act could be agreed upon under certain hypothetical conditions. See 155, 176, and 315.
[16] Although Scanlon does not explicitly characterize his view as a version of moral constructivism, he does claim that his view is a version of what Korsgaard calls 'procedural realism'. See 380, note 48. According to Korsgaard's characterization, procedural realism is the view that 'there are answers to moral questions *because* there are correct procedures for arriving at them.' By contrast, 'the substantive moral realist thinks that there are correct procedures for answering moral questions *because* there are moral truths or facts with exist independently of those procedures, and which those procedures track' (Korsgaard 1996: 36–7).

individuals specified in terms of their motivation and the process of reasoning they employ. Nonrejectable principles are not, on this picture, merely evidence for true or correct moral principles; there are no agreement-independent principles. Rather, the truth or correctness of moral principles is constituted by the fact that they are agreed upon in the specified circumstances.

In section 4, we return to some of the details of Scanlon's contractualism. First, let us consider a generic challenge to the sort of view Scanlon favors.

3. An old dilemma: Indeterminacy or relativism

The dilemma is a familiar one, often used to challenge nonrelativist versions of moral constructivism, as well as versions of moral contractualism, and the combination of the two.[17] In this section, I will state the dilemma and then in the following three sections I will return to Scanlon's view with an eye to whether he is able to avoid it.

Versions of moral constructivism typically impose certain constraints on the conditions under which some moral judgment or moral principle is true or correct. Either those constraints are relatively morally neutral and thus non-question-begging with respect to competing normative moral theories (and competing moral principles) or the constraints involve substantive, non-neutral moral assumptions. Call the former, 'morally thin' characterizations of truth or correctness and call the latter 'morally thick' characterizations. (Of course, a characterization may be more or less thin, more or less thick.)

If the characterization is morally thin, no substantive normative questions are begged, but we get serious indeterminacy. For example, if we characterize the relevant notion of justifiability as one in which moral deliberators select moral principles on the basis of certain available factual information and make no nonmoral mistakes in their reasoning about which principles to accept, then one can only expect some vague and indeterminate moral principles will be selected as a result of the process of moral

---

[17] Constructivism is also haunted by a version of the Euthyphro dilemma. For an excellent presentation of the objection, see Shafer-Landau 2003: ch. 2. For an attempt to come to grips with this dilemma, see Hill 2001.

reasoning so characterized.[18] (See the next section for some elaboration of this claim.)

On the other hand, if the characterization of the conditions under which a moral principle or judgment is justifiable is morally thick and thus includes substantive normative claims and assumptions, then moral relativism seems unavoidable. After all, when we load the account of justifiability with one set of moral assumptions, we get one particular set of 'true' moral principles, and we get alternative competing sets of 'true' moral principles when we load the account with alternative competing moral assumptions. If the constructivist is less ecumenical in viewing the many alternative 'true' sets of moral principles and insists that one or the other of them constitutes moral truth while the others do not, the burden is on her to point to some feature of the favored construction that could explain this difference in status. The problem is that there does not seem to be any non-question-begging feature to which the constructivist can help herself in breaking symmetry among the various competing sets of constructed principles.

Thus, the account of justifiability that figures in the constructivist's account of moral truth, whether thin or thick, yields an implausible metaethical view.

4. Avoiding indeterminacy

One of the main challenges, then, to any moral theory that attempts to account for morality by appealing to a notion of rational or reasonable agreement is to specify a substantive notion of rationality or reasonability figuring in moral thinking that will yield a fairly determinate set of moral principles. Formal constraints on such reasoning – consistency, completeness, and the like – are (taken together) too weak for purposes of specifying some reasonably determinate set of moral principles. But also, to require that such reasoning be *impartial* or reflect *equal respect* for

---

[18] Michael Smith's (1994) version of moral constructivism has serious problems with indeterminacy. Smith analyses moral judgments about rightness (obligation) as judgments about what all hypothetically rational agents would desire, and characterizes rationality (in the realm of choice and action) in morally neutral terms. For a criticism of Smith's view that charges it with objectionable indeterminacy, see Horgan and Timmons 1996b.

all individuals is also too weak to have much constraining power. This point is well put by James Griffin:

> Every moral theory has the notion of equal respect at its heart: regarding each person as, in some sense on an equal footing with every other one. Different moral theories parlay this vague notion into different conceptions. Ideas such as the Ideal Observer or the Ideal Contractor specify the notion a little further, but then they too are very vague and allow quite different moral theories to be got out of them. And the moral theories are not simply derivations from these vague notions, because the notions are too vague to allow anything as tight as a derivation.[19]

Scanlon's contractualist account of moral reasoning can be seen as filling out a notion of moral impartiality (reflecting a conception of equal respect for persons) by specifying the relevant notion of reasonability – a notion that is supposed to capture a morally relevant notion of justifiability.[20] So at the center of Scanlon's contractualism is a complex and nuanced account of moral reasoning that features the notion of *reasonability*. Judgments about what is and is not reasonable to do or to think (1) are made in relation to some given specified aim and (2) are relative to relevant available information and a relevant range of reasons (both of which may be less than complete).[21] In relation to moral reasoning, Scanlon's notion of reasonability presupposes the shared aim of finding principles of mutual self-governance that can be justified relative to a body of relevant available information and a set of relevant reasons. Principles (and the actions they mention) that are justifiable from this perspective are principles that no one could reasonably reject. Thus, filling out this

---

[19] Griffin 1986: 208 (see also 231 and 239).

[20] As I see it, the notion of reasonability in Scanlon's work represents a specification of the more general notion of justifiability.

[21] Scanlon (22–33) distinguishes judgments of rationality from judgments of reasonability. Judgments of rationality have to do with whether there are systematic connections between what an agent takes herself to have reasons to believe, feel, or intend and her beliefs, feelings, and intentions. Thus, 'irrationality in the clearest sense occurs when a person's attitudes fail to conform to his or her own judgments: when, for example, a person continues to believe something . . . even though he or she judges there to be good reason for rejecting it, or when a person fails to form and act on an intention to do something even though he or she judges there to be overwhelmingly good reason to do it' (25). See also Sibley 1953 and Rawls 1993: 38–54 for a contrast between rationality and reasonability very similar to Scanlon's.

contractualist account of reasoning requires specifying in some detail what counts as relevant information and relevant reasons, and doing so in a way that captures a distinctively contractualist notion of impartiality.

As Scanlon develops his view, reasoning about what we owe to each other focuses primarily on considerations that count as personal reasons – reasons having to do with the well-being, claims, and the status of *individuals*, rather than impersonal reasons having to do with things of value other than persons, such as other species and the environment (219).[22] Again, Scanlon's view requires that the kinds of reasons that figure in proper moral reasoning be *generic*: 'reasons that we can see that people have in virtue of their situation, characterized in general terms, and such things as their aim and capabilities and the conditions in which they are placed' (204).[23] How are relevantly motivated individuals supposed to reach agreement based on facts about the generic personal reasons of various individuals? This brings us to the heart of Scanlon's account of moral reasoning.

The procedure of moral thinking that Scanlon describes is thoroughly *holistic* and driven by *intuitive judgment having moral content*. It is holistic in the sense that reasoning about competing principles in arriving at conclusions about which action in some circumstance is justifiable requires that we appeal to relevant background moral principles and assumptions. '[A] sensible contractualism . . . will involve a holism about moral justification: in assessing one principle we must hold many others fixed' (214).[24]

---

[22] The exclusion of impersonal reasons is, for Scanlon, definitional: the category of what we owe to each other has to do with reasons implicated in the value of human beings – reasons that have to do with their well-being, claims, and status. 'By definition, impersonal reasons do not represent forms of such concern' (219–220).

[23] This requirement reflects limits on human cognition. No one can be expected to reason in light of the various particular aims and reasons of all individuals who would be affected by principles of mutual governance. Humans are obviously limited in their knowledge about others. Moreover, the principles reached as conclusions of moral reasoning are meant to guide moral reflection and choice and so must be manageable in terms of their complexity. Thus, because of human cognitive limits and the intended role of such principles in our lives, moral reasoning must rely on commonly available information about the general kinds of reasons people have in various types of circumstances. For some discussion of this issue, see 170–71, 204–6, 255, and 263. However, in various places in his book Scanlon notes the tension in particular cases between a pressure to refine moral principles (in order to accommodate more specific features of an individual's circumstances) and a counter pressure to formulate principles in more general terms. See esp. 205 and 255.

[24] Scanlon considers and rejects foundationalist forms of contractualism that would attempt, for example, to specify a nonmoral notion of welfare as well as a procedure for

Furthermore, in thinking about which generic personal reasons are relevant in some context and what sort of rational weight they have, we must rely on our intuitive judgment – moral judgment: 'the judgment that *any* consideration constitutes a relevant, possibly conclusive, reason for rejecting a principle in the context of contractualist moral thinking I am describing is a judgment with moral content' (217).[25] Based on holistic, judgment driven reasoning, Scanlon defends a *nonwelfarist* view about the kinds of generic personal reasons that can be morally relevant in determining the justifiability of an action – reasons that may include considerations of the welfare of individuals, but may also include reasons having to do with the moral claims of individuals (e.g., claims having to do with fairness) and their status as individuals. Furthermore, the manner in which such personal reasons figure in moral thinking represents, on Scanlon's account, a nonaggregative, *distributive* conception[26] of the process of justification according to which 'the justifiability of a moral principle depends only on various *individuals'* reasons for objecting to that principle and alternatives to it.' (229). Bringing together these various elements of Scanlon's view, we can make the initial formulation of his notion of rightness (expressed above by S2*) more precise as follows:

S3 An action is right if and only if it is distributively justifiable to all relevantly motivated individuals based on personal generic reasons, including but not limited to considerations of individual welfare.

Scanlon's nonwelfarist conception of relevant personal reasons distinguishes his contractualism from any form of utilitarianism, while his distributive conception of moral reasoning distinguishes his view from any form of consequentialism.

So here is where we are. In order to fend off worries about indeterminacy, Scanlon works with a robust, morally loaded conception of justifiability on the basis of which he argues for fairly determinate moral principles regarding, for example, promising and responsibility. But the price of determinacy is

reasoning about welfare from which one could reach substantive moral principles. See Morris (1996) for a defense of foundationalist contractualism.
[25] For related comments, see especially 141 and 194–5.
[26] I borrow the apt phrase, 'distributive justifiability' from Pettit 2000a and 2000b.

some form of objectionable relativism, or so I will proceed to argue.[27]

5. Relativism and chauvinism[28]

The main claim of this paper is that Scanlon's constructivist contractualism is not able to avoid one or another form of objectionable relativism despite his claims and arguments to the contrary. In order to defend this claim, it will help if we briefly consider two kinds of relativism and why they are (or may be) objectionable.

What I call *standard relativism* is the view that within some mode of discourse there is a (perhaps implicit) relativization parameter at work, so that in cases where, for example, two individuals are making what might appear to be claims that are directly contradictory, their claims are not really directly contradictory and they may in fact both be making true claims. Definite descriptions, for example, plausibly represent a type of discourse involving the kind of relativization parameter in question. The referent of a definite description, from among a set of eligible referents, is determined largely by contextually operative parameters that involve some kind of relativization. One party says 'The mayor has just been defeated in the election' and the other party says 'The mayor has not just been defeated in the election'. Both parties may be right if they are referring to the mayors of two different cities. In ethics, views that would construe moral terms and concepts as involving an implicit relativization parameter of a certain sort are versions of standard moral relativism. These versions of moral relativism involve a metaethical view according to which: (1) the proper semantic working of basic moral terms and con-

[27] Someone optimistic about working with a relatively non-morally loaded conception of justifiability might attempt to appeal to noncontroversial concrete moral judgments (e.g., torturing innocent peoples for fun is wrong) in addition to more or less formal constraints on moral justifiability in order to reach the kinds of substantive judgments and principles about a wide range of cases calling for moral judgment. Again, I don't think this ploy will deliver the moral theorist from objectionable indeterminacy. For instance, a consequentialist and a contractualist will agree about the morality of a range of fairly concrete moral judgments, but they will nevertheless differ significantly on many everyday cases of the sort featured in, for example, ethics advice columns. (Thanks to Terry Horgan for discussion of this point.)
[28] This section borrows heavily from Horgan and Timmons 1996a: sec. 3.

cepts involves an implicit reference to the moral norms or principles of some actual or hypothetical group, (2) the semantic constraints on such terms and concepts do not uniquely select one single group whose norms or principles determinately fix the truth of moral claims, and thus (3) apparently incompatible moral statements made by different individuals or groups can both be true.[29]

A more radical form of relativism – *conceptual relativism* – involves the claim that what appear to be conflicting and directly contradictory claims about a single subject matter involve terms and concepts which, although they may appear to be the same are in fact so different as to not be intertranslatable. Consider, for instance, interpretations of scientific discourse according to which there is 'radical incommensurability'. For example, if one held that earlier and later claims about electrons are conceptually incommensurable and hence not directly at odds with one another, then one would be espousing a strong conceptual relativism about the meaning of 'electron'. A more plausible example of conceptual relativity is exhibited in the semantic construal of natural kind terms advocated by Putnam and Kripke. The natural kind term, 'water' as used by people on earth, because its referent and meaning are tethered to empirical facts about the stuff that fills the oceans and falls from the sky here on earth, differs in reference and meaning from the natural kind term 'water' as used by twin earthings from Twin Earth. Given the Putnam/Kripke construal of 'water', this word is not directly translatable from one language into the other.

In ethics, a version of conceptual relativism would be committed to the idea that when two individuals or groups make apparently contradictory moral claims and thus appear to have genuinely conflicting moral views about some subject matter, they are not really disagreeing at all because the 'moral' terms and concepts they are using are not really intertranslatable; they are talking past one other.

From the nonmoral examples used in explaining these two forms of relativism, it is clear that some modes of discourse are properly understood as involving terms and concepts for which a relativist treatment is entirely plausible. However, let us say that a version of relativism, for a certain class of terms and concepts, is

---

[29]   David Wong (1984) defends a version of standard relativism.

chauvinistic just in case it entails that in cases where two individuals or groups really do seem to be thinking or uttering contradictory judgments employing those terms and concepts, the judgments in question are not really contradictory at all. Typically, an important source of evidence that some version of relativism is chauvinistic is when there is a mismatch between what the theory says about certain cases one the one hand and what pretheoretic common sense says about those cases on the other. In particular, we have evidence of chauvinism when common sense says that certain judgments really are contradictory and we have a genuine case of disagreement, whereas the theory says that there is a lack of genuine disagreement, either because the terms and concepts involved are not intertranslatable (conceptual relativism) or because despite sameness of terms and concepts, the claims in question have different truth conditions (standard relativism).

Now I submit that relativistic treatments of moral terms and concepts are chauvinistic and thus we have reason (defeasible, of course) to reject versions of moral relativism.[30] I won't defend this claim here and in any case, Scanlon would agree. But I maintain that Scanlon's constructivist contractualism commits him to chauvinistic moral relativism *malgré soi.*

6. Conceptual relativism?

Unfortunately, Scanlon does not expound a moral semantics for 'right' and 'wrong' (in the narrow senses of these terms).[31] However, it is clear from what he does say about the nature of the property of wrongness, that the moral concepts in question (and the terms that express them) are concepts that pick out a certain substantive property of justifiability to others. One way to under-

---

[30] Granted, a nonrelativist view in ethics can allow for what is often called 'circumstantial relativism' (what Scanlon calls 'parametric universalism'), but the kinds of moral relativism under consideration here are not simply of this variety; they represent the idea that moral thought and discourse is properly treated as 'deeply' relativistic. The distinction between deep moral relativism of the sort Scanlon wants to avoid and allowable circumstantial relativism is discussed further in section 8 below.

[31] Regarding different semantic interpretations of reasons judgments (e.g., belief views versus expressivist views), we noted earlier that Scanlon proposes to stay neutral. The main lesson of this paper is that he can't remain neutral, but needs to embrace a metaethical account of the meanings of moral terms and concepts that both secures his contractualism while avoiding relativism.

stand the specification of these concepts (and corresponding properties) is to view Scanlon as building directly into the concepts the type of non-welfarist, non-consquentialist moral theory he favors. But if we understand Scanlon's specification of the relevant concepts in this manner, the result is conceptual moral relativism. Let us explore further.

Recall from section 4 the formulation of Scanlon's main principle of rightness that specifies the kind of nonwelfarist distributive justifiability featured in his particular contractualist moral theory.

> S3 An action is right if and only if it is distributively justifiable to all relevantly motivated individuals based on personal generic reasons, including but not limited to considerations of individual welfare.[32]

One way to understand this property identity is to view it as implied by the concept of moral rightness that Scanlon develops. This interpretation results from (1) building into the very concept of moral rightness some fairly determinate normative outlook O_s in such a way that (2) to use the word 'right' in a way that incorporates some alternative and conflicting normative outlook O_p entails that two parties engaged in an apparently genuine moral disagreement (one making judgments employing O_s and the other employing O_p) are not disagreeing at all; in fact they are not really employing the same normative concept in their respective uses of 'right'. But, as explained in the previous section, this would represent a chauvinist version of conceptual moral relativism. To see how this kind of view would work out in relation to Scanlon's morally loaded version of constructivism, let us consider a dispute between a consequentialist and Scanlon.

Here I think it will be illuminating to consider Philip Pettit's reaction to Scanlon's view. Pettit is a consequentialist, who suggests that the property that Scanlon is really theorizing about is not moral wrongness, but a distinct property which he calls civility:

---

[32] As Terry Horgan pointed out to me, even though distributiveness is built into S3, there is a prima facie worry about indeterminacy in connection with this principle. After all, there are competing, distribution-sensitive moral theories that comply with S3 and going from S3 to some particular distribution-sensitive moral theory will require additional moral input.

I acknowledge that Scanlon's [contractualist] test picks out a salient moral category . . . I argue only that that category is not co-extensive with rightness, in any important sense . . . What Scanlon draws to our attention, as I see it, is that equally there is a code that all of us implicitly master when we learn the practice of relating to one another in the manner of reason givers and reason takers: in the manner best exemplified by the relationship assumed when people converse with one another on a noncoercive, nonmanipulative basis. Scanlon does better than anyone before him in marking the fact that this code – this code of civility – is inscribed in our most basic expectations as to how others will treat us and in our assumptions about how they will expect us to treat them.[33]

One way of viewing the dispute between Pettit and Scanlon is to suppose that Pettit and Scanlon are working with different concepts which they express by their respective uses of the words 'right' and 'wrong'. And this analysis of their dispute (at least suggested if not endorsed by Pettit) involves a commitment to conceptual moral relativism. But if we understand their dispute in this way, then when Pettit, in conformity with his consequentialist perspective, says of some act of lying that it is right and Scanlon, in conformity with his nonconsequentialist perspective, says that the act in question is not right (wrong), they aren't engaged in a genuine disagreement because (on the current reading) they are employing different terms expressing different concepts – terms and concepts that are not intertranslatable.

Now it may be (though I doubt it) that Pettit and Scanlon are theorizing about different properties for which they both use the words, 'right' and 'wrong'.[34] But the point I am making here is that it would be a mistake to propose an account of the semantics of moral terms and concepts which would entail this result. And this result is entailed if we understand Scanlon's constructivist account of moral terms so that Scanlon's particular nonconsequentialist moral outlook is built right in to the very concepts of right and wrong.

---

[33]   Pettit 2000a, 163–4. See also Pettit 2000b.

[34]   On might think that Pettit's remarks here are beside the point because Scanlon is only theorizing about the morality of what we owe to each other and not about the entire scope of moral concern. So, of course, Scanlon's term 'right' is not coextensive with moral rightness. (I thank Ken Westphal for raising this concern.) I understand Pettit to be saying that even if we restrict our concern to the morality in the narrow sense, Scanlon's concept of right is not coextensive with rightness in regard to what we owe to each other.

7. Standard relativism?

However, one need not understand Scanlon's view in this way and there is textual evidence that Scanlon rejects it.

> I argue that contractualism provides the best interpretation of what at least many of us are claiming when we say that an action is morally wrong. But I am not offering it as an account of the meaning of the word 'wrong' or of the expression 'morally wrong'. These terms can be used by people who hold non-contractualist accounts of morality, such as utilitarianism, divine command theories, and it would not be plausible to claim that in such cases these words are being misused or have a different meaning. (9–10)

Now one way to accommodate these claims about sameness of meaning and thereby avoid conceptual moral relativism is to interpret moral terms and concepts as involving an implicit relativization parameter so that proper uses of terms like 'right' and 'wrong' involve reference to some fairly determinate moral outlook or other. Let me explain.

Suppose we allow that the core of the concept of wrongness is captured by a set of moral platitudes, including S1 – the claim that wrong actions are actions that are not justifiable. Other platitudes include such claims as: *the rightness or wrongness of an action (when it comes to what we owe to each other) is concerned with such considerations as being fair, relieving need, being honest and so forth; if one action is right and all of the other available actions are wrong, then one ought to perform the right action; wrong actions are actions one has reason to avoid and reason to criticize others for performing.* One can certainly add to this list of platitudes.[35] Arguably, the relevant set of platitudes does not yield a determinate concept of wrongness or of rightness – a number of competing moral theories are fully compatible with such platitudes. But suppose we understand the concept of wrongness and rightness so that their semantical working is similar to that of 'flat' in the sense that at a course-grained level, when a consequentialist and a contractualist use terms like 'right' and 'wrong', they are using the same terms

---

[35]   The last item on this list is mentioned by Scanlon in the passage that I quoted earlier from p. 12 of Scanlon's book. See also Pettit (1997: 107–8) for a list of fifteen such features, including the ones I've just mentioned.

(expressing the same concepts).[36] However, such terms and concepts (let us suppose) involve as part of their proper semantical working, an implicit relativization parameter, so that in using these terms (and concepts) to make determinate moral judgments, one employs some normative outlook or another which fixes the conditions under which the judgment is true. This allows that when Pettit and Scanlon make apparently conflicting claims about some act of lying, they are employing what is in some sense the same moral concepts expressed by the terms 'right' and 'wrong'.

However, the resulting view is a version of standard moral relativism. Given that Pettit's use of these terms involves an implicit reference to and use of his particular version of consequentialism, while Scanlon's use of those same concepts involves reference to and use of his particular version of contractualism, their apparently conflicting claims may both be (relativistically) true. Again, although this sort of view allows us to say that Scanlon and Pettit are (at a course-grained level) employing the same concepts of rightness and wrongness, nevertheless this sort of view yields a form of standard moral relativism, and such views are, as we have noted, objectionably chauvinistic.

So here is where we are. Scanlon seemingly offers us a morally loaded version of constructivism – he seems committed to loading a particular nonconsequentialist, distributivist version of contractualism into his metaethical construal of such terms and concepts. It would seem that either he does so in a way that yields a version of chauvinistic conceptual moral relativism or, perhaps more likely, he does so in a way that yields a version of chauvinistic standard relativism. Either way, his view involves a kind of moral relativism that is at odds with his attempt to defend moral objectivity. Or so it seems.

8. Chauvinistic relativism avoided?

Scanlon denies that his view is or entails the kinds of chauvinistic moral relativism I have been describing. In order to reinforce the

---

[36] For some discussion of concepts that involve contextually variable parameters in relation to the phenomenon of conceptual relativity, see Horgan and Timmons 2002.

relativist worry that I have been pressing, let us consider what he has to say about avoiding relativism.

His main defensive strategy, developed in the last chapter of his book, is one of accommodating within his view a significant degree of moral variation without the view collapsing into a form of objectionable moral relativism. This accommodation strategy itself involves two main tactical ploys. First, Scanlon claims that some variations in moral standards have to do with moral concerns that fall outside the narrow core of morality which is concerned with what we owe to each other. For example, there would appear to be deep variations in personal ideals – ideals of personal honor and excellence – that represent multiple and incompatible values that are worthy of adoption and which thus support conflicting standards of conduct. Since Scanlon's philosophical project is focused exclusively on considerations of what we owe to each other, conflicting ideals and standards regarding areas of morality outside this narrow scope, do not pose a relativist threat to contractualism.

Scanlon's second tactical ploy is to explain, within the limits of his moral contractualism, admissible types of moral variation. Some admissible variation in moral judgment and practice can be explained by the fact that universally correct moral principles have different implications about right and wrong when applied in different sets of factual circumstances. This familiar kind of variation – Scanlon calls it 'parametric universalism' – is clearly compatible with the rejection of relativism at the level of basic moral principles.

Again, Scanlon proposes to explain other cases of permissible variation by appealing to variations in the generic personal reasons people have owing to facts about their social situation. Scanlon illustrates this tactic in relation to the value of privacy. For instance, differences in prevailing social conceptions of personal dignity across societies as well as differences in particular forms of commercial and other transactions, give people in different societies different general reasons for favoring certain specific principles of personal privacy.

Now I don't think these ways of accommodating variation are enough to avoid the charge of objectionable relativism. Indeed, Scanlon's accommodation ploys are useful for zeroing in on the kinds of cases – cases of 'moral symmetry' – that are most troubling for a moral constructivist. These cases involve the following stipulations: (1) two individuals or groups are engaged in a moral disagreement over some issue or case, (2) because they are placed in circumstances that are as similar as possible, their disagreement is not explicable owing to the kinds of differences appealed to in Scanlon's second ploy, (3) the individuals or groups are plausibly interpreted as making no factual errors in relation to their moral judgment about the case at hand, (4) their respective moral outlooks enjoy wide reflective equilibrium, and hence (5) their respective moral views on the topic in question are stable. In some of the papers I have co-authored with Terry Horgan, we have considered cases of moral symmetry involving a mythical place we call 'moral Twin Earth'. A moral Twin Earth scenario involves imagining two groups, one on earth whose moral judgments are in a state of stable wide reflective equilibrium and are captured by some non-consequentialist deontological moral theory T^d, while the moral judgments of twin earthlings are also in a state of stable wide reflective equilibrium but captured by some conse-quentialist moral theory T^c. We have used moral Twin Earth sce-narios in pressing our objections to various 'new wave' forms of moral realism that attempt to make use of various semantic and associated metaphysical views of recent vintage in defending moral realism.[37] The important upshot of our moral Twin Earth arguments against versions of moral realism is that, depending on the particular version of semantic moral realism on offer, they are all impaled by one horn or the other of the indeterminacy/ objectionable relativism dilemma. Moral constructivism has the same problem, which can be brought out in the same sort of way – by reflecting on cases of moral symmetry.

In the dispute between Scanlon and Pettit, we already have the basis for constructing a suitable moral Twin Earth example. But we need not travel to Twin Earth to work the argument based on cases of symmetry, because we have a nicely articulated example from the writings of Putnam:

> One of my colleagues is a well-known advocate of the view that all government spending on 'welfare' is morally impermissible.

---

[37] Richard Boyd (1988), for instance, defends a version of moral realism by making use of the semantic construal of natural kind terms defended in the work of Kripke and Putnam. Horgan and I criticize Boyd's view and the views of other realists such as David Brink (1989) and Peter Railton (1993) in Horgan and Timmons 1992, 1996a, and 2000b. As we explain – see esp. our 1996 and 2000b – our moral Twin Earth argument represents a *recipe* for criticizing forms of moral realism and so, for example, it works against realist semantic proposals in metaethics that do not construe basic moral terms as being seman-tically analogous to natural kind terms as the latter are understood by Kripke and Putnam.

On his view, even the public school system is morally wrong. If the public school system were abolished, along with the compulsory education law (which, I believe, he also regards as an impermissible government interference with individual liberty), then the poorer families could not afford to send their children to school and would opt for letting the children grow up illiterate; but this, on his view, is a problem to be solved by private charity. If people would not be charitable enough to prevent mass illiteracy (or mass starvation of old people, etc.) that is very bad, but it does not legitimize government action.

In *my* view, *his* fundamental premises – the absoluteness of the right to property, for example – are counterintuitive and not supported by sufficient argument. On *his* view I am in the grip of a 'paternalistic' philosophy which he regards as insensitive to individual rights. This is an extreme disagreement, and it is a disagreement in 'political philosophy' rather than merely a 'political disagreement'.[38]

Here we have a case in which two philosophers have thought through various implications of their own moral outlooks, have gotten clear about the morally relevant details of the case, and have, on the basis of reflecting about the relevance and weight of generic personal reasons representing various individual standpoints, come to conflicting moral judgments over the issue of welfare spending. These kinds of symmetry cases can be easily multiplied, and they present a problem for any moral constructivist. In relation to Scanlon's version, the problem is that relative to one kind of moral sensibility, certain generic personal considerations are going to count as relevant and certain specific judgments about the various weights of reasons are going to count as reasonable.[39] We get convergence among all appropriately motivated individuals *who happen to share a certain moral sensibility* – one like Putnam's. But we also get convergence among all appropriately motivated individuals who *happen to share a different moral*

---

[38]   Putnam 1981: 164.

[39]   In various places throughout his book, Scanlon indicates that his version of contractualism is anchored in moral judgments that he and like-minded individuals find intellectually appealing. 'The contractualist view I have presented appeals to me because it offers an account of a central part of morality that fits with our, or at least my, moral experience – that is to say with my understanding both of the content of moral requirements and of the reasons supporting their authority' (351–2).

sensibility – one like Nozick's. If moral truth is a matter of what all
hypothetical agents would agree to under certain specified conditions, and those conditions involve a morally loaded notion of
rationality or reasonability, then in light of symmetry cases we are
committed to some form of objectionable moral relativism. Either
we have to say that at the end of the day Putnam and Nozick (or
Pettit and Scanlon) are employing different 'moral' concepts and
so they are talking past one another (conceptual moral relativism)
or their respective uses of moral terms like 'right' and 'wrong'
have importantly different truth conditions (standard moral
relativism). Can Scanlon's view avoid this implication?

In the final section of his chapter on relativism, Scanlon considers cases of deep moral disagreement (although he does not
work with a developed example). Here is what he says about them:

> According to contractualism, disagreements about the wrong-
> ness of an action often come down to disagreements about
> the relative weight of the reasons that people in various posi-
> tions have for rejecting principles that would license or permit
> such actions. Disagreement thus often arises from the fact that
> we often do not have, or do not bear in mind, a sufficiently
> clear idea of how people occupying different positions would
> be affected by different moral requirements. Partly as a result,
> we are apt to exaggerate the cost to us of departures from what
> we are accustomed to expect, and to minimize the costs to
> others that may make it reasonable to demand such changes
> (358).

Failure to properly consider the effects of various competing
moral principles on those individuals who will be affected by
them, then, is one source of moral disagreement, perhaps leading
to the sort of deep disagreement described by Putnam. And
Scanlon suggests other reasons for such disagreement, including
the complexity of specific moral issues as well as such distorting
psychological factors as self-interest, partisanship, lack of sufficient imagination and careful analysis in moral thinking.

Now I can't prove that both Putnam and Nozick have sufficiently clear ideas of how people occupying different roles would
be affected by their favored principles, nor can I prove that one
or the other of them has otherwise failed in some way in their
moral thinking about welfare spending. But I think such diag-
noses of the dispute are rather desperate in this case. And anyway,
the kind of hypothetical case of moral disagreement featured in

Twin Earth and other such scenarios, make it reasonably clear
that two individuals or groups can disagree, yet neither party is
guilty of excessive self-interest, lack of imagination, lack of sufficient factual information and the rest.

Return for a moment to Scanlon's constructivist moral metaphysics and the sort of view about moral terms and concepts that
such constructivism apparently implies. I have argued that according to one way of construing such concepts, the view ends up as
a version conceptual moral relativism: 'moral' terms and concepts
as used by a contractualist are different terms and concepts from
those used by a noncontractualist. I have also argued, that according to an alternative way of construing them that allows for sameness of terms and concepts, the constructivist position ends up
embracing a version of standard moral relativism. Finally, to reinforce this verdict, I have considered Scanlon's various ploys for
avoiding objectionable relativism, and argued that reflecting on
cases of moral symmetry reveal that in the end they aren't enough
to combat the charge of moral relativism.

9. Nonconstructivist contractualism?

What I take to be Scanlon's moral constructivism plays a relatively
minor role in his overall contractualist moral theory – a substantive nonconsequentialist normative moral theory. As explained
above in section 1, a moral contractualist need not be a moral
constructivist, there are other metaethical views about moral
ontology and truth that are available. Let me briefly mention a
few of these options – options one might think would avoid relativism – and indicate why, on their own, they are not plausible.
Here, I will not be able to fully argue my case, but I refer the
reader to other writings for support.

Most obviously, Scanlon might embrace a form of moral
realism and thus claim that principles that cannot be reasonably
rejected are evidence of independently existing moral facts.
Defending this kind of view would require developing a moral
semantics to undergird the moral ontology. But if it can be done,
then Scanlon would have a nonrelativist basis for his contractualism. Unfortunately, the prospects for moral realism look rather
dim. In our articles that I've previously mentioned, Terry Horgan
and I have criticized various forms of moral realism arguing that
attempts to develop an appropriate moral semantics lead one way

or the other to relativism. Our various Moral Twin Earth arguments make use of cases of moral symmetry in showing this result. But behind all of these various arguments is a *recipe* that we think one can use to cook up an appropriate case of moral symmetry that will be the undoing any version of moral realism.

I have already noted that Scanlon hopes to avoid commitment to moral realism. But another metaethical option would combine (1) realism about reasons for action with (2) a kind of constructivism about *moral* reasons.[40] The idea is that there are stance independent facts about which considerations are and are not reasons for action. However, not all such considerations are morally relevant in a particular context. Their relevance and relative force as moral reasons are determined by the results of a process of moral reasoning – let it be the one Scanlon proposes. Would this kind of mixed metaethical view help the cause of the nonrelativist moral constructivist? I think it is fairly clear that it won't. First, one must defend realism about reasons for action, and there is reason to suspect that it will prove to be as difficult as defending moral realism. But second, even if realism about reasons could be defended, the same old problems we have seen in connection with moral constructivism will apply directly to the kind of constructivism on offer here. From the perspective of a clear-headed consequentialist, the kinds of reasons that are morally relevant and their rational force will differ enough from the kinds of reasons a clear-headed nonconsequentialist will take to be morally relevant and possess a certain rational force. We seem to be right back in the lap of the moral relativist.

Another type of metaethical view that countenances substantive moral properties is a dispositional view according to which moral properties are analogous to secondary qualities like color properties. On this sort of view, the claim that something is good is analyzed in terms of the reactions of standard observers under standard conditions. Thus, 'good' picks out those properties of

---

[40] In various places in his book, Scanlon claims that one of the main functions of his contractualist account of moral reasoning is to explain which considerations in some given context are morally relevant. '[T]he "shaping" role of the aim of justifiability to others is a dynamic one. There is no fixed list of "morally relevant considerations" or of reasons that are "morally excluded." The aim of justifiability to others moves us to work out a system of justification that meets its demands, and this leads to a continuing process of revising and refining our conception of the reasons that are relevant and those that are morally excluded in certain contexts' (157). See also 218. Scanlon would seem to be committed to holism about moral reasons – a view of reasons that is central to the sort of moral particularism defended by Dancy (1993, 2004).

items of evaluation that are the objects of the kinds of reactions featured in the analysis of the concept of goodness. The result is a response-dependent account of moral properties and facts, but an account that purports to deliver a robust notion of moral objectivity.[41] However, this view comes to grief for much the same reason that response-independent versions of moral realism come to grief: when the semantic account underlying the metaphysical view of moral properties is spelled out, the view succumbs to relativism.[42]

In the end, I don't believe there is hope for a substantive account of moral properties and facts that will underwrite a nonrelativist metaethical view. Nor do I think we should embrace moral relativism.

10. A proposal: Metaethical minimalism

Suppose, then, that we reject moral constructivism. And suppose we reject other metaethical views that countenance substantive moral properties and facts. I said at the outset that I think that some of the main elements of Scanlon's contractualism can be nevertheless preserved. What I have in mind is a type of minimalist metaethical view that can accommodate some elements in question without collapsing into objectionable relativism. I won't able to fully develop the kind of view I have in mind, so my remarks will necessarily be rather sketchy. But for a fuller articulation and development of metaethical minimalism, I refer the reader to some of the work that Terry Horgan and I have published.[43] First the sketch and then I will return to Scanlon's contractualism.

The view can be set forth in a series of seven related tenets:

1. Minimalism maintains that moral thought and discourse, because it has all of the logico-grammatical trappings of genuine assertoric thought and discourse, is indeed genuinely assertoric. To form a moral judgment is to form a

---

[41] Advocates of the dispositional view include Johnston (1989), Wiggins (1991), and McDowell (1998).

[42] This claim is forcefully argued by Sean Holland (2001), who makes use of moral Twin Earth scenarios in developing this criticism.

[43] See especially, Horgan and Timmons 1994 and 2000a, and also Timmons 1999: ch. 4.

genuine belief whose content is appropriately expressed in declarative moral sentences that possess genuine asserotic content. This represents a form of metaethical *cognitivism*.

2. However, moral beliefs and sentences are not descriptive – they do not purport to represent or describe robust moral facts of some sort. Rather, they are in the business of guiding ones attitudes and actions. The view thus represents a *non-descriptivist* metaethical view.

3. The view is semantically minimalist because it refuses to give any kind of deep analysis – reductive or nonreductive – of moral thought and discourse. According to this view, the proper response to a question such as 'What is the content of a sentence like "Apartheid is wrong"?' is a minimalist one: 'Apartheid is wrong'.

4. However, this is not a version of metaethical quietism: there is genuine illumination to be gained about moral thought and discourse, but it comes mainly from understanding the point and purpose of such thought and discourse and by understanding the distinctive functional role of moral belief in human cognition. Thus an adequate account of the point and purpose of moral assertions and of the cognitive-functional role of moral beliefs, will be one in which various subtle decision-guiding and action-guiding aspects of moral beliefs and moral judgment are made perspicuous.

5. The view is also ontologically minimalist because it does not countenance any metaphysically robust moral properties or facts, including constructed properties and facts. It is a robust form of moral irrealism.

6. However, truth ascriptions are quite legitimate and should be understood minimalistically according to Tarski's schema T. The semantic remark that, for example, ' "Apartheid is wrong" is true' expresses a moral commitment to the claim that apartheid is wrong from within a morally charged metalinguistic stance.

7. Finally, this version of metaethical minimalism is not a form of moral relativism. It does not offer a relativized account of the contents of moral beliefs and utterances, nor does it construe moral judgments as involving an implicit relativization parameter or otherwise give an account of reference and truth that entails moral relativism. So, for instance, when one utters a logically simple moral claim such as 'Apartheid is wrong', one is not to be understood as making a statement

that has some hidden relativization parameter that would make the statement turn out to have relativized truth conditions. Moral beliefs and utterances are typically *categorical*.

Horgan and I began working out this view some time ago, calling it 'assertoric nondescriptivism',[44] later calling it 'nondescriptivist cognitivism'. Recently, John Skorupski has defended a view about normativity that combines the idea that normative judgments have truth-assertible cognitive content, but 'there are no worldly facts in virtue of which pure normative propositions are true when they are true.'[45] Skorupski calls his view, 'irrealist cognitivism' and in basic outline it is a close cousin of the metaethical view that Horgan and I favor. We believe that this kind of metaethical view, when fully spelled out, does not require the positing of any metaphysically substantive moral properties or facts, and does not land us in the lap of the moral relativist.

With this sketch in hand, let us return finally to Scanlon's moral contractualism. Following standard characterizations of moral constractualism, I presented it as an epistemological view according to which the justification of moral principles and judgments depends on the outcome of some agreement, whether actual or hypothetical. I also distinguished formal from substantive contractualism, the latter representing a particular view about the justification of moral principles that incorporates non-consequentialist moral ideas.[46] Perhaps the two most central ideas in Scanlon's substantive contractualism are these:

1. Interpersonal agreement over principles governing what we owe to each other ought to guide moral theorizing, and
2. Moral theorizing ought to recognize the importance of non-aggregative modes of moral thinking in arriving at principles that can meet with interpersonal agreement.

These normative claims represent general moral claims reflective of a particular moral outlook. Understood from the point of view of the metaethical minimalist, they represent categorical moral

---

[44] Horgan and Timmons 1994, Timmons 1999, and Horgan and Timmons 2000a.
[45] Skorupski 2000: 116–7.
[46] Note that as an account of justification, formal contractualism is faced with the kind of indeterminacy/relativism dilemma raised in connection with constructivism: either the account of justification is morally thin in which case we get indeterminacy regarding the justification of moral principles and judgments, or we get relativism about justification if the account is morally loaded.

assertions – assertions that one might hope to defend through a process of moral reasoning. To make sense of moral reasoning and the claims such reasoning aims to support, we need not (and should not) understand moral judgments as descriptive of some moral properties and facts, whether such properties and facts are stance independent as a realist would have it or stance dependent as a constructivist would have it.

11. Conclusion

I have argued that Scanlon seems to embrace what I have called a version of constructivist contractualism and I have focused in particular on the constructivist part of this package, arguing that at the end of the day it is committed to one or another form of objectionable moral relativism. I maintain that in order to avoid relativism, Scanlon ought to reject constructivism as well as any metaethical view that would commit him to substantive moral properties and facts. Rather, I propose that a minimalist meta-ethical view can provide the appropriate metaethical underpinning that will allow Scanlon to avoid relativism and preserve the main elements of his moral contractualism. This latter claim is controversial and would require far more philosophical investigation than can be accomplished in a single article. But in any case Scanlon needs some metaethical underpinning (in the form of a semantic account of moral judgments) for his moral contractualism if he hopes to make sense of moral thought and discourse while avoiding relativism.[47]

References

Brink, David, O. (1989). *Moral Realism and the Foundations of Ethics* (Cambridge: Cambridge University Press).
Boyd, Richard (1988). 'How to be a Moral Realist' in Sayre-McCord (ed.), *Essays on Moral Realism* (Ithaca: Cornell University Press).
Dancy, Jonathan (1993). *Moral Reasons* (Oxford: Blackwell Publishers).
—— (2004). *Ethics without Principles* (Oxford: Oxford University Press).
Griffin, James (1986). *Well-Being* (Oxford: Oxford University Press).
Hill, Thomas E., Jr. (2001). 'Hypothetical Consent in Kantian Constructivism', *Social Philosophy & Policy* 18: 300–29.

[47] I wish to thank Justin Fisher, Terry Horgan, Russ Shafer-Landau, Ken Westphal, and the audience at the University of Arizona for their very helpful comments on an earlier version of this paper.

Holland, Sean (2001). 'Dispositional Theories of Value Meet Moral Twin Earth', *American Philosophical Quarterly* 38: 177–95.

Horgan, T. and Timmons, M. (1994). 'Taking a Moral Stance,' unpublished ms presented at *Hare's Heritage: The Impact of R. M. Hare on Contemporary Philosophy*, The University of Florida, Gainesville, FL.

—— (2002). 'Conceptual Relativity and Metaphysical Realism', *Philosophical Issues* 12: 74–96.

—— (2000a). 'Nondescriptivist Cognitivism: Framework for a New Metaethic', *Philosophical Papers* 29: 121–53.

—— (2000b). 'Copping Out on Moral Twin Earth', *Synthese* 124: 139–52.

—— (1996a). 'From Moral Realism to Moral Relativism in One Easy Step', *Critica* 28: 3–39.

—— (1996b). 'Troubles for Michael Smith's Metaethical Rationalism', *Philosophical Papers* 25: 203–31.

Johnston, Mark (1989). 'Dispositional Theories of Value', *Proceedings of the Aristotelian Society* 63: 139–74

Korsgaard, Christine (1996). *The Sources of Normativity* (New York: Cambridge University Press).

McDowell, John (1998). 'Values and Secondary Qualities' in *Mind, Value, and Reality* (Cambridge, Mass.: Harvard University Press).

Milo, Ronald (1995). 'Contractarian Constructivism', *The Journal of Philosophy* XCII: 181–204.

Morris, Christopher W. (1996). 'A Contractarian Account of Moral Justification' in Walter Sinnott-Armstrong and Mark Timmons (eds.), *Moral Knowledge?: New Readings in Moral Epistemology* (New York: Oxford University Press).

O'Neill, Onora (2003). 'Constructivism vs. Contractualism' in Philip Stratton-Lake (ed.), *Ratio* XVI (4).

Pettit, Philip, Baron, M. W. and Slote, M. (1997). *Three Methods of Ethics* (Oxford: Blackwell Publishers).

Pettit, Philip (2000a). 'Two Construals of Scanlon's Contractualism', *The Journal of Philosophy*, 148–64.

—— (2000b). 'A Consequentialist Perspective on Contractualism', *Theoria* LXVI: 228–36.

Railton, Peter (1993). 'Noncognitivism about Rationality: Costs, Benefits, and an Alternative', *Philosophical Issues* 4, 36–51.

Rawls, John (1980). 'Kantian Constructivism in Ethics', *The Journal of Philosophy* 77, 515–72. Reprinted in J. Rawls, *Collected Papers*, Samuel Freeman (ed.), (Cambridge, Mass.: Harvard University Press, 1999).

—— (1985). 'Justice as Fairness: Political Not Metaphysical', *Philosophy and Public Affairs* 14, 223–51. Reprinted in J. Rawls, *Collected Papers*, Samuel Freeman (ed.), (Cambridge, Mass.: Harvard University Press, 1999).

—— (1993). *Political Liberalism* (New York: Columbia University Press).

Sayre-McCord, Geoffrey (2000). 'Contractarianism' in Hugh LaFollette (ed.), *The Blackwell Guide to Ethical Theory* (Oxford: Blackwell Publishers, Inc.).

Scanlon, T. M. (1998). *What We Owe to Each Other* (Cambridge, Mass.: Harvard University Press).

—— (2000). 'A Contractualist Reply', *Theoria* LXVI, 237–45.

Shafer-Landau, Russ (2003). *Moral Realism: A Defense* (Oxford: Oxford University Press).

Sibley, W. M. (1953). 'The Rational versus the Reasonable', *The Philosophical Review* 62, 554–60.

Sinnott-Armstrong, Walter (1996). 'Moral Skepticism and Justification', in W. Sinnott-Armstrong and M. Timmons (eds.), *Moral Knowledge? New Readings in Moral Epistemology* (Oxford: Oxford University Press).

Skorupski, John (2000). 'Irrealist Cognitivism' in J. Dancy (ed.), *Normativity* (Oxford: Blackwell Publishers).

Smith, Michael (1994). *The Moral Problem* (Oxford: Blackwell).

Timmons, Mark (1999). *Morality without Foundations: A Defense of Ethical Contextualism* (New York: Oxford University Press).
Wiggins, David (1991). 'A Sensible Subjectivism?' in *Needs. Values. Truth.* (Oxford: Basic Blackwell).
Wong, David (1984). *Moral Relativity* (Berkeley: University of California Press).

7

REPLIES

T. M. Scanlon

Onora O'Neill, Derek Parfit, Joseph Raz, Mark Timmons, and Jonathan Wolff raise many challenging questions about my book. It is a privilege to have such thoughtful critics. I cannot deal adequately with all of their questions here, but I will try to say something about the central issues that each of them raises.

As O'Neill notes, I take the idea of a reason as primitive. That is to say, I do not try to explain what it is for something to be a reason. Nor do I try to state substantive 'rational constraints' on what reasons for action there are. This does not make the concept of a reason that I am employing 'thin' or 'weak.' Using this concept, one can make judgments drawing whatever distinctions there are between those considerations that are (good) reasons for action and those that are not. Perhaps O'Neill has in mind that spelling out a *conception* of reasons for action would involve specifying 'rational criteria' determining which things are such reasons and which are not. Like anyone else, I have views about which considerations are reasons for action, and I make many judgments of this kind in the course of my argument. But I doubt whether it is possible to state general criteria from which these judgments (let alone all valid judgments about reasons for action) follow. (This is one of several ways in which I am not a Kantian.) If this is what O'Neill has in mind by a conception of reasons for action then I am not providing such a conception (weak or otherwise.)

O'Neill may see the notion of a reason that I employ as 'weak' because she does not notice that I distinguish between a reason for action (a consideration that *in fact* counts in favor of some action) and what I call an agent's 'operative reason' for an action (a consideration that an agent *takes* to count in favor of so acting.) *Taking* something to be a reason for action may, as she says, be 'a pro-attitude directed towards action falling under some description.' (28) But *reasons* for action are not, in my view pro-attitudes.

The idea of a reason is often thought to be less clear than the ideas of desire and motivation. I have come to hold the opposite

view. The idea of motivation seems to me an unstable combination of a purely psychological idea (a state that causes action) and
a normative one (a consideration that makes action rational.)
'Desire' is commonly used in what is said to be a broad sense, in
which any 'motivating state' counts as a desire. But it is nonetheless also generally assumed that desires in this sense provide
reasons for action. This seems to me a mistake. When one acts on
a desire, what generally provides one's reason for action is some
feature of the thing desired, not the desire itself. Here again there
may be some confusion between reasons for action and an agent's
operative reason (what he or she takes to be a reason) for acting
in a certain way. Since having a desire generally involves seeing
some consideration as a reason for acting, a person's desire may
determine what his or her operative reason for acting was. But
even so, it is not the desire itself that is the agent's reason. When
I desire to go indoors because it is cold outside, my reason for
going in is my discomfort (and the fact that going in will relieve
it) not the fact that this is what I desire. Perhaps O'Neill is correct
that, given these views, I should have avoided the terms 'desire'
and motivation' altogether.

O'Neill raises questions about whether my view is contractualist or constructivist in the sense in which she understands these
terms. Contractualists, she suggests, 'ground ethical or political
justification in *agreement* of some sort, whereas constructivists
ground them in some conception of a reason.' (19) As she goes
on to acknowledge, this way of drawing the distinction 'does not
provide any neat separation of the two approaches to justification.' A theory may, as mine does, ground ethical claims in claims
about what individuals have *reason* to agree to, in which case it is
not clear which of the approaches it represents. As I understand
her, O'Neill goes on to mark a clearer distinction between
contractualism and constructivism as she understands them by
taking contractualism to ground justification in *de facto* contingent agreement. I take this to be indicated by her remark that
Rawls's method of Reflective Equilibrium is contractualist because
it "assumes that 'we' agree on certain considered judgments."
(20)[1]

Claims about reasons figured in two ways in the argument of
my book. First, in order to defend claims about the content of

---

[1]   I would not interpret Reflective Equilibrium in this way. For my views on this see
'Rawls on Justification,' in Samuel Freeman, ed., *The Cambridge Companion to Rawls*, (Cambridge: Cambridge University Press) 2002, pp. 139–167.

morality, according to my version of contractualism, one needs to make claims about the reasons that individuals have for accepting or rejecting certain principles as standards of conduct. Second, I claimed that we have reason to care about the justifiability of our actions to others and that this is a central reason for our concern with the morality of our actions. This emphasis on what principles others have reason to accept (or reject), and on our reasons for caring about this, led me to call my view 'contractualist.' But it is not a contractualist view in O'Neill's sense of the term, if I understand her correctly, since neither of the two kinds of claims about reasons that I have just mentioned is grounded in any contingent agreement. What people do, as a matter of fact, agree to (like what individuals have, as a matter of fact, consented to) can be morally relevant in certain cases. But neither actual agreement or actual consent plays a fundamental role in morality as I describe it.

I agree with much of what Jonathan Wolff says about well-being. He does, however, take my aims in Chapter 3 of *What We Owe to Each Other* to have been more ambitious, and aggressive, than they in fact were. My intent in that chapter was not 'to cut utilitarianism off at the knees, by arguing that there is no notion capable of playing the role that utilitarianism needs.' (33) What I argued that we are unlikely to find is an account of well-being that is, at the same time, a notion that is central to the deliberation of the individual whose life is in question and a notion that captures the way in which benefits and burdens for that individual should be measured for the purposes of moral or political argument. From an individual's own point of view, I argued, the boundaries of well-being are essentially unclear. My reasons for concluding this were as follows.

Success in one's main aims (insofar as these are rational) is an important component of well-being. An individual's reasons for pursuing his or her aims are not, however, mainly ones of well-being. (This is not to say that these aims must be impersonal, as Wolff sometimes seems to suggest. They may include such things as benefiting one's children, for example.) But while success in these aims makes one's life better, there is no clear answer to the question of how much it does so. Suppose I have sacrificed my comfort and many other pleasures in order to give my children a better life. How would we go about deciding whether my success in doing this did or did not offset the sacrifice involved, leading to a net gain in well-being? I doubt that such questions have, in general, any clear answer. But the more important point is that such an answer is not needed, either from an individual's own perspective or for the purposes of a moral theory or theory of justice.

From the individual's own perspective the question is whether the sacrifice in comfort and other pleasures is worth it, given the benefit to his or her children. This is an intelligible question, but not I argued, a question about his or her well-being, understood as 'how well a life goes, from the point of view of the person whose life it is.'

For the purposes of a moral theory, or a theory of justice, we need a way of measuring benefits and burdens that draws a reasonably sharp line between what counts and what does not. There are many such notions, and consequentialist, or utilitarian, theories, as well as non-consequentialist theories can make use of them. The choice among such notions should, however, be based on their suitability to the moral task at hand, not on the degree to which they capture some pre-moral notion of well-being. For example, what social choice theories take as inputs are individuals' preferences over all states in the 'domain.' This may include individuals' preferences over things that are too far removed from their lives to be plausibly seen as affecting their well-being. The fact that preference satisfaction is in this respect much broader than well-being is no objection, however, if the choice of which elements in this domain society is to pursue is a choice that individuals, as citizens, are entitled to have a role in making. Similarly, Rawls's notion of primary social goods and Sen's capability sets measure much less than 'how well a person's life goes.' This is, in itself, no objection to them. The claim made on their behalf is not that they measure well-being but that they capture the aspects of individuals' situations that a theory of justice should be responsive to. Perhaps neither of these notions succeeds in doing this, and an adequate measure needs to reflect more fully the degree to which a person is successful in achieving his or her main aims. If so, however, the question to be answered in devising an alternative is the moral question of how just social institutions must aid individuals in the pursuit of their aims, not the pre-moral question of the degree to which success in an aim (in providing for one's children, for example) contributes to a person's own well-being.

I agree with Raz in taking the idea of a reason to be the fundamental practical concept, and I agree as well with much of what he goes on to say about reasons. There are, however, a few points of disagreement that I should note.

First, Raz holds that 'reasons [for action] consist in the fact that actions possess certain evaluative properties making them worth performing, etc., or bad, etc.' I would say rather that although the properties of actions that make them worth performing are in some cases evaluative properties, this is not always the case. Ordinary natural properties of actions can also be reasons for performing, or not performing them. Second, it seems to me somewhat strained to speak of reasons as 'calling for compliance.' It seems to me rather that they count in favor of, or against courses of action. But since I believe they can do so conclusively, perhaps this disagreement is merely verbal.

The first of these disagreements may lead to another. Raz holds that 'reasons (and values) are inherently intelligible,' meaning by this that 'it is possible to explain why any specific reason is a reason.' (56) I also think that reasons are inherently intelligible, but I doubt that it is always possible to explain, in other terms, why something is a reason. Raz may think this is always possible because a reason (at least a reason for action, which is the kind under discussion) can always be explained by citing the evaluative property on which it is based. I, on the other hand, believe that evaluative properties often need to be explained by citing reasons. For example, the claim that something is good is made intelligible by citing the properties, often non-evaluative ones, that give us reason to pursue it, promote it, or whatever.

Do I hold that there is a single 'master argument which establishes the validity of all moral reasons?' This depends on what one means by 'moral reasons.' I am a pluralist about morality and hence about moral wrongness in the broadest sense of this term. But I do offer a form of argument for establishing that an action is wrong in one particular way (a violation of what we owe to each other.) If the property of being wrong in this way provides a reason not to perform an action (a question I will say more about presently), then this argument uniquely establishes that we have that kind of reason not to perform an action. I believe that when people say that an action would be wrong they believe that it contravenes standards that there is good reason to treat as authoritative, but they may not have a very clear idea what these reasons are. So when people who have never heard of contractualism conclude than an action is wrong they may have in mind some reason against it that is different from what contractualism describes. But they may also be referring, perhaps somewhat unclearly, to the kind of reason that it does describe. So people who call actions wrong without having heard of contractualism may, but need not, have been constructivists *manqués*. (56)

I turn next to Raz's charge that my contractualism is vacuous because 'its test yields results only by presupposing moral views which can only be established independently of it.' (58) In applying contractualism one must appeal to intuitions about what can reasonably be rejected. These intuitive judgments are guided by some interpretation of the central contractualist idea of justifiability to others.

I interpret this idea as requiring that reasons for rejecting a principle must be 'generic reasons' that any person would have in virtue of standing in one of the positions in a situation of the kind to which the principle applies (for example, the position of a person to whom assurances have been given, or that of the person who gave these assurances, or that of a third party affected by whether these assurances are kept.) These must be reasons that such a person would have 'on his or her own behalf.' This interpretation, which embodies what Parfit calls my 'Individualist Restriction,' rules out, as grounds for rejecting a principle, appeals to impersonal values, such as the intrinsic value of preserving the Grand Canyon, or to aggregate benefits. What it allows are reasons arising from the way a person would be affected by following the principle, or by having others do so. These may include not only considerations of well-being, but also such things as the reasons one has to want outcomes to depend on one's choices, and the reasons one has to object to being treated arbitrarily, or having one's central interests not taken into account.

This is not a complete specification of the possible reasons for rejecting a principle. As we consider more cases we may find other considerations that seem clearly to be relevant grounds for objecting to principles. Nor, as Raz notes, does it provide a standard for assessing the relative strength of reasons for rejecting a principle and opposing reasons for insisting on it. One must simply judge whether certain considerations do or do not provide sufficient grounds for rejection.

In so doing we are making intuitive judgments about answers to particular kind of question that contractualism identifies as relevant to questions of right and wrong. Insofar as what we are doing is *applying* some particular interpretation of contractualism, however, we will not base these judgments on independent judgments about what is right or wrong. But of course one also has views about this, and in some cases they may conflict with the conclusions that contractualism seems to lead to. When this happens (as in some aggregation cases, which I will discuss in a moment) one needs to consider, on the one hand, whether this moral intuition seems on reflection to be sound and, on the other hand, whether the version of contractualism that leads to the conclusion in question should be modified or rejected.[2] This 'reflective equilibrium' process is what is going on in the second part of Parfit's contribution to this volume. In the first part he is applying contractualism as I interpret it (observing what he calls the 'moral beliefs restriction'). In the second half he is arguing that that interpretation should be modified by dropping the individualist restriction. As he observes near the end of the paper, in order to maintain that this is a reinterpretation rather than an abandonment of contractualism, he needs to argue that I was mistaken in thinking that this restriction follows from the guiding idea of justifiability to others. Similarly, when I said that an argument giving greater weight to numbers than my version of contractualism allows is 'not excluded in advance' by the general idea of contractualism I meant to be leaving the door open to the possibility of a reinterpretive argument of this kind.[3] But some reconciling argument is needed to show that it is not in fact excluded.

Aggregation poses a serious challenge for contractualism, but not in the way that Raz suggests. The problem is not one of vacuousness but something closer to its opposite: that conclusions that appear to flow from a natural way of understanding reasonable rejectability conflict with clear moral intuitions. Interpreted in the most straightforward way, contractualism seems to rule out aggregation in cases like the life-saving example that Raz discusses, cases in which aggregative reasoning seems clearly correct

[2] This is not, however, what was going on in the passage Raz cites from pages 208–209. There I claimed that a principle that would in general discount harms suffered by only a few people is one that could reasonably be rejected. In so doing, I was relying on an intuitive judgment about reasonable rejection As Raz observes in a footnote (note 12) recognizing this possible response, I did not offer any argument for this intuition. None seemed to me to be needed, since the reasonableness of rejecting a principle that would, in general, license the infliction of severe harms on a few for the sake of small benefits to others seemed to me obvious.
[3] The remark is from p. 241 of my book, quoted by Raz on p. 66.

and appears to be the only way of reaching the obviously right answer. The question this poses is whether there is a way of understanding the grounds of reasonable rejection that would get the intuitively correct result in these cases, but would not be ad hoc, or in conflict with other elements of contractualism. I am not sure that the 'tie-breaking' argument which I offer, and which Raz examines, meets this test. But the fact that a parallel argument could be offered outside the contractualist framework is no objection here. The challenge for contractualism is to overcome the objection that it rules out plausible aggregative arguments. To do this it would be sufficient to show that familiar non-contractualist arguments can be plausibly recast in contractualist terms. There is no need to claim that this argument is uniquely contractualist.

I turn now to Parfit's discussion of aggregation. At one point in his paper he writes, 'We now have four views to consider. On Scanlon's Individualist Restriction, different people's burdens cannot be morally summed. On the Tie-breaker View, when we must choose whom to save from equally great burdens, numbers can break ties. On the Close Enough and Disproportional Views, great burdens can be outweighed by many lesser burdens that are close enough in size, but these lesser burdens have disproportionately less weight.' (78)

Since I did not propose the Disproportional View, and Parfit does not favor it either, I will set it aside. Parfit argues that, contrary to what I maintained in my book, the Tie-breaker View is not compatible with the Individualist Restriction. He says that in the life boat case, White could reject the Tie-breaker view and insist on getting an equal chance of being saved. More generally, Parfit says that if my Individualist Restriction is maintained, then 'Whenever we could give equal benefits either to some people or others, we ought to give everyone an equal chance of getting these benefits, since that is always what would make the greatest individual burden as small as possible.' (76–7) This conclusion seems to me to show that there must be something wrong with Parfit's argument for using the Equal Chances Principle in cases like lifeboat, since it would require one to give each person an equal chance of a benefit no matter how sound the argument may be for giving a benefit to one of them rather than the other.

The problem lies, I think, in a failure to take into account the different ways in which we may 'give people chances' of certain benefits. Certainly there are cases, like Parfit's medical example, in which, due to lack of information about the consequences of the actions open to us, the best we can do is to give people a certain chance of benefiting, and we must decide on that basis. The lifeboat example is not a case of that kind: we can choose to save White or to save the five, and in the end we will choose one of these courses or the other. Flipping a coin enters just as a way of deciding which to do. In some cases this may be the fairest way to decide. Whether it is or not will depend on whether there are good substantive grounds for directly choosing one course or the other. So one needs first to determine what the available grounds are, and what they support. This is what I meant by saying that in such cases (where ignorance is not a factor) we should consider the ultimate stakes for the people affected.

Even if the Tie-breaker View is consistent with the Individualist Restriction, it can explain only a few of the cases in which aggregative arguments seem, intuitively, to be morally relevant. As I acknowledged in my book, there are other plausible cases that it cannot explain. Parfit argues forcefully that in order to explain those cases the Individualist Restriction must be dropped. He suggests that, 'In rejecting some principle, each person could appeal to the burdens that this principle would impose not only on her, but also on other people.' (87) He maintains that a view that allowed this would still be distinctively contractualist. This change would, he argues, strengthen the theory. Raz, on the other hand, maintains that allowing aggregation would deprive contractualism of any distinctive content. Which of them is correct? The answer to this question seems to me to depend on the way in which elements of the resulting view restrict aggregative arguments, thus avoiding implausible results in cases such as that of Jones and the transmitter. More exactly, it depends on whether these elements have a clear contractualist rationale.

One such element on which Parfit suggests we should rely is the Priority View. As Parfit states it, this view holds that 'benefiting people matters more, the worse off the people are to whom these benefits would go.' For reasons that will become clearer later, I think the view would be better stated in terms of reasons for rejection: the worse off people would be if they are not benefited, the stronger their reasons to reject principles that would deprive them of these benefits. Parfit's examples involving weeks of future pain illustrate the appeal of this principle. In Case Two, where the baseline is equal, benefiting only Blue seems objectionable, because all have the same claim to some benefit;

whereas in Case One, Blue's claim to some treatment is much stronger than the others' since the prospect he faces if untreated is much worse.

Applied to the Transmitter case, the Priority View would say that even though we must consider the sum of the small costs to those who would be deprived of entertainment for a short time as a reason against a principle requiring the transmitter to be turned off to spare Jones, his reason for wanting the transmitter turned off still makes it unreasonable to reject this principle. His reason is stronger than the aggregate of theirs because he would be much worse off if not benefited.

If, on the Priority View, the unequal baseline just means that Jones' reasons are made somewhat stronger than they otherwise would have been, it may seem that this reason could be outweighed by the aggregate reasons of some larger number of television viewers. But it seems to me that there is no such number: we should spare Jones no matter how many viewers there are. To explain this conclusion while allowing aggregation we would need to supplement the Priority View with something like the Close Enough View, perhaps in the form that Parfit calls the Triviality Principle. He believes that this principle should be rejected. Even very small benefits should not be ignored, he argues. They must be taken to count for something in order to explain why we have reason to participate in schemes that provide goods (or prevent harms) to others even when the difference that our action makes to each of the affected persons is very small.

I take a different view of these cases. Suppose, for example, that an action of a certain type can be avoided only at significant cost to the agent and, if performed once, will impose trivial costs on each of a large number of people. But if actions of this type are performed frequently, the costs to each of these others add up and become very significant—greater (for each victim) than the cost (to each agent) of avoidance. There are many actions of this type. In such cases, it seems clear to me that the permissibility of the action depends on whether a restraining principle is needed—that is to say, on whether there is good reason to believe that, in the absence of some principle of restraint, such actions will be widely performed. So I would endorse the Triviality Principle in the qualified form that Parfit mentions at the end of his section 4.

Parfit believes that a version of contractualism that admits aggregative reasons and includes the Priority View and other dis-

tributive principles remains contractualist and is even a stronger
view of that type. His reasons for thinking this may be as follows.
The Priority View (at least as I have reformulated it) is just a claim
about factors affecting the relative strength of reasons in interpersonal justification. Since contractualism must rely on such
claims in any case, this addition does not weaken it. Since the
resulting view avoids implausible implications, contractualism is
strengthened by this change. Moreover, the Priority View (and,
one might add, the Close Enough View, and other distributive
principles) is most naturally understood within the context of a
view that makes conclusions about right and wrong depend on
the relative strength of the reasons that individuals can offer in
the process of interpersonal justification. By comparison, these
principles make much less sense as elements of a utilitarian or
other consequentialist doctrine. They are less plausibly interpreted as claims about what it is good or bad to have happen. So
these non-contractualist views are less able to provide convincing
explanations of the limits of aggregative justifications.

Raz might reply that this defense rests on taking utilitarianism
as the alternative. He might say that contractualism should be
compared instead with a view that takes moral conclusions simply
to be conclusions about the relative strength of reasons, along the
lines sketched in the first part of his paper. The Priority View, or
the other principles Parfit advocates could, he might say, be
equally well understood in these terms, simply as claims about the
relative strength of reasons, dispensing with the contractualist
packaging, which adds nothing.

I, at least, and I assume Parfit as well, would deny that the contractualist framework adds nothing. Morality is drained of its
special significance if it is taken to be simply about the relative
strength of the reasons that there are. It is important, in order to
account for the special significance of moral conclusions, to recognize that what is at stake are the reasons we can offer one
another in a process of mutual justification.

Timmons is correct that my version of contractualism is not
what he calls 'formal contractualism,' since it does not leave open
the normative content of first order morality. But my view is not
substantive in the particular way Timmons describes. It is not a
view according to which 'a moral principle is justified only if *each
individual* (who is part of the relevant justifying agreement) either
does or would agree to the principle in question.' There are, as
Timmons points out, a few points in my book at which I refer to

my view as involving a hypothetical agreement. But this was care-lessness on my part. At most of those points I was, quite correctly, contrasting my version of contractualism with a view that bases morality on principles that everyone *actually* accepts (or, I might have said, principles that no one *actually* rejects.) But it would be a mistake to say that what is fundamental in my view is therefore hypothetical *agreement*. What is basic in my view is what no one *could reasonably* reject, not what certain people do or hypo-thetically would agree to (or not reject) under some specified conditions.

This difference may seem small, but it is of fundamental impor-tance. Claims about what people would or would not reject under certain conditions are most naturally taken to be descriptive claims, not normative ones. I would not have suggested that we identify claims about moral wrongness with non-normative claims. I suppose that claims about hypothetical agreement (or non-rejection) might be understood as normative claims, say about what people would agree to, or would not reject, insofar as they were reasonable. But on this construal the hypothetical char-acter of the claim would be idle. All the real work would be done, as in my view, by straightforwardly normative claims about what people could reasonably reject (or refuse to agree to.)

My version of contractualism does, however, have substantive moral content. This gives rise to possible objections of two sorts. The first is the charge of circularity. I address this charge in my book, and will not repeat that response here.[4] The second objec-tion, which I will discuss, concerns the issue mentioned by Derek Parfit in the final footnote of his contribution to this volume, namely whether what I offer should be understood as an account of the property of moral wrongness or an account of what makes acts wrong. This is connected with problems that Timmons raises about how moral disagreement is to be understood on my view. I agree that there is a problem here, but for reasons that I will explain it does not seem to me to be properly described as a problem about relativism.

I did not take myself, in my book, to be offering an account of the meaning of the English expression 'morally wrong.' I imagine that the meaning of 'morally wrong' is something like, 'open to serious criticism because it violates standards of conduct that

---

[4]   pp. 241–247.

REPLIES 135

everyone has good reason to regard as authoritative.' A plausible
account of the meaning of 'morally wrong' should not have specific moral content built into it. For one thing, this expression is
properly used to cover a wider range of objections than those
having to do with 'what we owe to each other.' Moreover, even
within this domain it can be used, without linguistic oddity, to
express many different moral views. People who use the expression 'morally wrong' to express different moral views can disagree
about the content of the standards they take to be violated or
about the reasons people have for taking these standards
seriously.

Accepting that an action would be morally wrong involves
taking oneself to have strong (normally conclusive) reasons not
to do it. But it does not follow that wrongness itself provides such
a reason. An action's being wrong may merely entail that other
considerations, apart from its wrongness, count strongly (normally decisively) against it. That is to say, wrongness may be what
I call a buck-passing notion.[5] But I supposed in my book that this
was not the case. I took it that the fact that an action would be
wrong is itself a strong, normally decisive, reason against doing it,
and I set out to characterize moral wrongness in a way that
explained how it could be reason-giving in this way. I recognized
that in doing this I could not be giving the meaning of 'morally
wrong' (or characterizing the concept of moral wrongness if this
is to be identified with the meaning of that expression) since, as
I have just said, people can use that expression non-deviantly even
if they disagree about what reason we have to take standards of
right and wrong seriously.

How, then, to describe what I was doing? In one sense it is perfectly clear what my project was. To claim that an action is wrong
is to claim that it violates standards that we have good reason to
take very seriously. What I was doing was to describe, in very
general terms, certain standards together with what I claimed was
a good reason for taking them seriously as ultimate guides to
conduct. My thesis was that these standards and this reason
provide the best way of understanding a large and central class of
cases of moral wrongness. This thesis was partly interpretive and
partly reformist. I offered it as a way of making sense of what many

[5] I argue in Chapter 2 of my book that goodness should be understood in this way. See
pp. 95–100.

of us believe when we say, in these cases, that an act is morally wrong, and also as an account of moral wrongness that people might endorse, on reflection, even if they had previously accepted some other understanding of the standards underlying their use of 'morally wrong.' I made it clear that what I was making was a substantive claim about moral wrongness (about what standards of conduct we should take seriously.) I also acknowledged that when some people claim that an action is morally wrong they may have in mind standards other than the ones I was describing, standards which they take to be authoritative for reasons other than the one I described, and that in some cases these reasons may be worthy of respect.

This ground level description of my project seems to me entirely correct, and I stand by it. Given that the contractualist formula was a substantive claim about wrongness, I might have described it as an account of what makes acts wrong, as Derek Parfit suggested to me at the time. I resisted this description for two reasons. First, that phrase seemed to me more properly used to describe properties such as harmfulness, in virtue of which actions violate moral standards. The fact that an action would cause harm may make it reasonable to reject a principle that would permit that action, and thus make that action wrong in the contractualist sense I am describing. It is also true that an action's being wrong in this sense makes it morally wrong in the perfectly general sense of that term, since being forbidden by the standards contractualism supports is one way of being forbidden by standards that there is reason to treat as authoritative. But these two ways of 'making an action wrong' seem to me rather different from one another. My second reason for resisting this description is that insofar as moral wrongness is taken to provide a reason for action, and contractualism aims to explain what this reason is, contractualism seemed to be a thesis about the normative status of moral wrongness, not just about what it took to give a particular action that status.

So, drawing on an analogy with natural kind terms, I presented contractualism as an account of the property of moral wrongness: as an account of the normative property that is shared by many of the actions we call morally wrong and accounts for their observed normative features, just as an account of gold aims to identify the physical property that is shared by observed instances of gold and explains their observed features. I pointed out (p. 13) that this analogy is imperfect. In the case of natural kinds, the property in question is unique (except in twin-earth type cases.) But as I acknowledged, this may not be so in the case of wrongness. When different people call actions morally wrong some of them may have in mind different standards, and different reasons that they take to support them.

Given that this is so, I should have avoided describing contractualism as an account of the property of moral wrongness. As Parfit and Timmons point out, doing so has the odd consequence that when a teleological utilitarian, or a divine command theorist says that an action is wrong, and a contractualist denies this, their disagreement does not consist in the fact that one side is affirming that the action has a certain property, and the other denying this. This does not mean, I would add, that the two sides are not disagreeing. They disagree about what standards we have most reason to take as ultimate standards for action, and one side is claiming, and the other denying, that the action in question violates such standards. This reply seems to me quite sound, as far as it goes, but conjoined with my earlier claims for contractualism it results in an odd divergence between the concept of moral wrongness and the property of wrongness. Applied to a case like the one just mentioned, this account describes the two sides as disagreeing about the applicability of the concept of wrongness to the action in question, but not in the properties they are claiming this action to have.

The claim to be describing the property of moral wrongness can be dropped from my account without affecting the other claims I make for contractualism. Perhaps I should describe my thesis instead as an account of what makes actions wrong. For reasons I have mentioned, however, this also strikes me as somewhat misleading. What is not misleading, and what I will stick with at present, is the ground level description given above. In the remainder of this reply I will take this as the basis for responding to some of Timmons's claims about disagreement and relativism.

It seems to me a strength of this ground level description of my project that it allows for several kinds of disagreement about right and wrong. First, people can disagree about what standards we should take as ultimate bases for assessing our conduct and that of others, and about the reasons supporting these standards. Second, given a shared conception of the relevant standards, people can disagree about what these standards in fact permit and require. My disagreement with Philip Pettit is best understood on the former model, as a disagreement about the reasons we have to take certain standards as guides to conduct. He takes the promotion of the best consequences as the ultimate basis on which standards of conduct should be justified. I disagree. It may be that we are 'theorizing about different properties,' but we are making conflicting claims about these properties and therefore not 'talking past one another.' He is trying to show how my idea of justifiability, which he calls civility, while it is not morally basic as I claim, nonetheless has a place within a consequentialist picture. I argue, on the other hand, that the idea of promoting the best consequences, while it is worthy of respect, should be subordinated to the idea of justifiability to others that I try to characterize. Different people may find one or the other side of this debate more convincing. But this does not mean that there is no answer to the question which of us is correct in the claims we make about the reasons people have.

People who agree about the general kind of justification that can and should be offered for standards of conduct may disagree in the second way I mentioned about what these standards in fact allow. So, for example, contractualists may disagree about the relative force of different reasons for rejection and hence about which principles it is reasonable to reject, and which actions are morally wrong. Again, it does not follow from the fact that people disagree in this way that there is no answer to the question which of them is correct. If we were to conclude in some case that there was no single correct answer, the result would be an instance of moral indeterminacy, not relativism.

Cases of disagreement in real life, such as that between Putnam and Nozick, may not be immediately classifiable as being of one or the other of the types I have just described. They may contain elements of both, and I believe that a good way to approach these disagreements is by trying to identify and distinguish these elements. This seems to me a more promising strategy than simply to suppose that there is one subject matter, 'morality' that they are making conflicting claims about.

INDEX

Fish, Stanley
  'The Unbearable Ugliness of
    Volvos' 40–1
Foot, Philippa 33
friendship 5

Gauthier, David 24
good
  see moral reasoning; wrongness
Greater Burden Principle 68–9
Griffin, James 101

Horgan, Terry 112, 115, 117,
  119

indeterminacy 138
  relativism and 99–100
  Scanlon and 100–4
Individualist Restriction 71–8, 87–8,
  128, 131
  Scanlon's anti-consequentialism
    79–83
  Scanlon's response concerning
    130
intuition 102–3, 128

justice
  Rawls and contractualism 22–4
justification
  Scanlon's contractualism and
    29–30; *see also* moral reasoning

Kant, Immanuel
  moral theory 33–4
  Rawls and 23
  social contract 19
Kripke, Saul 105

Locke, John
  social contract 19

Means Principle 68–9
metaethical theory
  constructivism and contractualism
    93–5
  minimalism 91, 117–20
  moral realism and 116–17
  quietism 94, 97
  Scanlon and 96
minimalism 91, 117–20

moral cases
  football transmission 11, 74, 132
  the lifeboat 75, 77, 87–8, 130–1
  the lifeguard 46–7, 53, 61–2
  painful diseases 79–81
  scarce medical resources 81–2,
    88, 131–2
  treating Green or Grey 76
  Twin Earths scenario 112–15, 116
moral realism 115–17
  metaethical minimalism and 118
moral reasoning
  act and rule consequentialism
    69–70
  benefits in proportion 82, 83–7
  Close Enough View 77–8, 79, 81,
    83, 133
  contractualism and 8–14, 55–6
  core argument about numbers
    53–5
  degrees of compliance 48–52
  Disproportional View 78, 81, 130
  division into three types 33–4
  equal value of individual lives 63
  'fault-making' 47
  filtering well-being preferences
    42–4
  indeterminacy 138
  Individualist Restriction 71–8,
    87–8, 128, 130, 131
  intuitive judgement 102–3
  as justification 16–17
  metaethical theory and 93–5
  mutual recognition 15–17
  normative 2–3, 26, 92–3, 134
  operative 2–3
  Parfit on Scanlon's formula
    67–72
  Priority View 14–17, 131–3
  public 22–3
  'reasonable' *versus* 'rational' 67
  reasons and motivations 123–4
  relativism 90–1, 138
  Scanlon's practical 28–31
  substantive good 6–7, 133–4
  symmetry 112–15
  testing contractualist claims 55–9
  thick and thin truth 99–100
  Tie-breaker View 74–5, 77–8, 130,
    131